The Way *of* Spirit

Teachings of Rose

Joanne Helfrich

NewWorldView
Topanga, California

NewWorldView
Topanga, California
www.newworldview.com

The Way of Spirit: Teachings of Rose
thewayofspirit.com

Cover Profile Photo: © J.A Rausch/Trevillion Images
Author Photo: Maureen Benoit
Cover Design: Joanne Helfrich

First Printing: December 2014
ISBN: 978-0982812334

Printed in the United States on acid-free, partially recycled paper.

10 9 8 7 6 5 4 3 2 1 4

" This marvelous book is easy to read and understand! Rose reminds us that humankind's true nature is essence, and as such, we are beloved aspects of All That Is. She reveals how it is essence's role to assist us to realize our dreams, fulfill our purpose, and recognize the deep interconnections between all the spirits who have served as humanity's teachers."

~ Joyce A. Kovelman, Ph.D.,
author of *Once Upon a Soul*

" Rose delivers rare and powerful insights into the process of spiritual evolution, and highly effective practices to encourage our own. After 30+ years 'on the Path' I'm grateful for her unique perspective. I had been looking right at some very important things without ever seeing them, and now I do! I guess this student was finally ready for her to appear."

~ James Bradford Terrell, co-author of
Emotional Intelligence in Action

" Rose, speaking through Joanne Helfrich, shows how we can all realize more joy and fulfillment in our lives by using our intuitive powers to become more fully in touch with our spiritual selves. The potential value of Rose's advice in daily living is substantially enhanced by the inclusion of a number of easy-to-follow exercises."

~ Alexander Astin, Ph.D., author of *Mindworks:
Becoming More Conscious in an Unconscious World*

Contents

you feel bad; Essence will tell you what your shadow is blocking; Others need you to *not* deflate their choices; You *shadow inflate* those you want to be; The ego is an important supporting player; Ego inflation and shadow inflation and suffering; Trust essence to relieve your suffering; Animals are your greatest teachers

For Jeanette and John Knapp—

*my mother, who taught me about spirit
through stories of sand dollars and
dogwood blossoms,*

*and my father, who taught me
through music.*

Foreword

R ose is, to put it mildly, an interesting personality. She describes herself as an *energy personality essence*—a multidimensional being who exists primarily outside our physical world of space and time. While we may consider her a singular personality and a "she", Rose refers to "herself" as "we"—a vast, collective, gender-inclusive energy that you can think of as spirit, soul, inner self, greater self, or *essence*.

She also refers to herself as a *Dreamwalker—an essence comprised of many essences who is directly involved with the creation and maintenance of physical reality.* In practical terms, she is a spiritual teacher, and a part of each of us, as we are expressions of essence that include physical and nonphysical aspects of experience.

While it's remarkable that Rose speaks to us in words, it's also unremarkable because we interact with essence in every moment whether we recognize it or not. Rose's objective is to help us each realize our direct connection with *our own* essence—which she also refers to as our Personal God—by embracing *The Way of Spirit,* and in doing so, live the most fulfilling life possible. That is why she provides the various practices in this book: to help us identify our unique, innate *intent—our essence's design for fulfillment—*and cultivate habits that help us live our most blissful, purposeful life.

Rose and I interact through my deep intuition, and I convey her words by autotyping, with my hands moving rather independently on my keyboard, and sometimes by speaking in a light trance state. The process employs a *bridge personality* in which an aspect of her energy merges with me to form a unique, temporary personality. As a result she can use my traits, vocabulary, and cultural framework to express her highly informed perspective on the nature of reality.

Because Rose is not my own essence, our interaction is sometimes referred to as an *energy exchange,* but the phenomenon is more widely known as *channeling.* Rose defines channeling as our *innate ability to accurately translate inner experience to outer experience* through artistry, healing, and other natural, inspired acts that align with our intent. This book will also help you connect with your own essence so that you, too, may learn to express your own special gifts in ways you may not have considered before.

While the abilities that I and others have to allow essence to speak through us in words may seem unusual, many scholars consider it a natural ability that has existed throughout history in expressions of divine revelation, prophecy, and transformative teachings such as those in the Bible and other spiritual and creative works. Each person translates inspired teachings according to their own beliefs and experiences, and every age has its own version of divine transmission that is pertinent to its time. In this, you may find that Rose's teachings are consonant with your own spiritual beliefs, and may press at the edges to expand and enhance them.

The way Rose speaks is sometimes wordy, but intentional…

"...to strike a chord in the readers that would be resonant with their sense of the spiritual. My use of your language is meant to provide a sense of sacred connectedness with the proud heritage that is yours in the way of spirit, which has always been communicated to you in sacred rather than secular ways. Therefore, *The Way of Spirit* will interest those who have been longing for the wisdom of the ancients to awaken their deepest, eternal selves, and to provide a modern update of the ancient teachings in terms you will find useful."

The Way of Spirit, therefore, evokes a rich lineage of inner knowledge that reflects our spiritual heritage—our birthright—that, if it is to be valuable, assists us in practical ways on our life's journey. It is a timely work, too, as we engage what many consider a global *shift in consciousness* in which we are opening more deeply to our essence selves on a mass level. The shift is changing the world daily and challenging each of us to evolve in new ways. Many of us need guidance on how we might do that. While we may aspire to big, permanent shifts, the way of spirit is about living in joy, not achieving perfection. Perhaps we only need to shift a little at a time—for a day, for an hour, for a moment.

On occasion, Rose uses neologisms—made up words—to help us break out of deeply held thoughts and beliefs (the Glossary will help you navigate new words and terms). For example, her word *feal* is a combination of *feel* and *real*—to feel most deeply, succinctly, and accurately. The word *senxual*, a combination of *sexual* and *sensual*, describes

"...the incorporation of scent, sound, taste, sensual pleasures such as a bowl of cherries, a sexual romp, a

most breathy view of your landscapes, a most breathy
view of your wonderful bodies, a scent on a tip of a
table lamp, a marvelous dinner, a most satisfying
martini."

Perhaps the most helpful thing about the teachings of Rose
is that they empower authentic transformation. While other
sources promote the idea that your life has purpose, few
actually help you to discover *yours*. The practices she offers at
the end of this book will help you do that.

Some of the ideas mentioned in this book may be new to
you, for example, that we create our physical reality through
our thoughts, beliefs, emotions, and expectations: that we
literally get what we concentrate on. Another is that all things
are part of God, the Universe, or *All That Is*. Consciousness,
which can be considered synonymous with Spirit or Divinity,
is primary in all of creation. While it's sometimes necessary to
describe levels of being, there are no closed systems or
divisions in Consciousness. (This also makes capitalizations
tricky! For practicality, capitalized words in this book
typically indicate the "God" level but are often relative.) As
such, reality is exponentially more vast, fluid, and
spontaneous than you may imagine!

That's all you really need to know about metaphysics to
gain value from this book. If you would like to know more, as
Rose mentions in the Introduction, the Seth Material by Jane
Roberts is the best contemporary source for in-depth
information about these and other ideas Rose discusses.

In the long run, how we get information isn't as important
as how helpful it is. As you read this book, use a discerning
mind and open heart to apply its ideas and practices. Your
direct experience will determine their validity and
transformational power. I believe with all my heart that in

doing so, you will discover whole new worlds within you. For more resources and information about Rose, visit **thewayofspirit.com**. For courses and other resources that integrate the most profound teachings of science, art, and spirit to help you realize your unique purpose in life, visit **newworldview.com**.

Acknowledgements

Many thanks to my partner Paul, and my many teachers including Jane Roberts, Seth, Elias, Kris, Dr. Don Beck, Ken Wilber, and Matthew Fox.

Thank you to those who have contributed to the Rose phenomenon from the beginning and through the publication of this book, including Chris W.E. Johnson, Frieda Corbit, Ellen Gilbert, Mark Bukator, David Tate, Nardine Neilson, Joyce Kovelman, Erin Collier-Plummer, Carol Hedeen, Lisa Green, Danny and Susan Scott, Daniel Scott Jr., Eric Helfrich, Celia Helfrich, Margot Evans, Bill Buonanni, Tom and Sharon Rose, Garry Corgiat, Barbara LeVan Fisher, Elena Kotliarker, and our many wonderful students, clients, and transcribers.

And special thanks to my friends who have courageously performed energy exchanges for years, set the bar high, and have been so inspiring and supportive—Mary Ennis and Serge Grandbois.

Joanne Helfrich
Topanga, California

Introduction

We are Rose, an *energy personality essence*. The *energy exchange* we perform with Joanne was intended to introduce you to yourselves, for in a sense you are Rose, and we are you. That is, we are a nonphysical aspect of you that serves as a teacher, and the way we teach is through what is called a *bridge personality* by Seth, who was introduced to your world by the late Jane Roberts.

You can learn more in your Seth books, so we will say for now that these are the gold standard, for Seth and Jane explored the channeling phenomenon in ways that provide mental, emotional, and spiritual information of great depth and utility. The Seth Material was dictated by Seth through Jane. This was not what your religious institutions call demonic possession, nor was this what your scientific institutions label a pathological psychological split.

The exchange was remarkable in many respects, not only with regard to the uniqueness of the phenomenon, but also in the way it skillfully promotes spiritual evolution when properly applied. The Seth Material reveals the ways in which spirit speaks to each of you in different stages of development. This book will help you develop your spiritual maturity, as will the Seth material and like resources, which we encourage you to read as well.

Now, you may think that you do not need spiritual maturity, but you may be incorrect. We suggest that you probably do, and that you would benefit from spiritual guidance. Your world is in many ways in jeopardy, and we can help you determine the fate of your planet, to preserve a home for generations to come. We know you care about this, so we will assist you, to assure your place in the world as protectors of your planet and the heroes of your own lives.

You are on a heroic journey

That's right! You are the heroes of your own lives. Joseph Campbell, the Jungian mythologist, was a wonderful teacher whom you may inform yourself of as well. His information was intended to make you aware that you are on your own heroic journey, and that you have latent heroic abilities. Your personal journey is intended to bring all of the challenges and rewards of your essence into your world.

Since you create all of your reality, it stands to reason that when you become the heroes of your own lives, you change yourself and your world for the better.

This can be seen in the *Star Wars* movies and other tales of heroic adventures. When you view these movies and read these stories, you see your own lives reflected in the hero's situation: you are destined to confront major issues, imbued with your own superpowers that make you the Jedi Knights and X-Men of your times. In your own way, you have stumbled upon a wise, Yoda-like teacher in Rose, to help you heed the call of your own hero's journey.

You *do* have an influential role to play in your world, and you *do* have an intent and purpose that you need to incorporate. We can help you do this through the information we will provide in this book. Allow us to help you develop your own heroic abilities and heroic self. Does that sound like fun? We hope so, for life was intended to be a fun adventure!

Essence is always here for you

Now, we are aware that you may have other questions about the channeling phenomenon to better understand who and what Rose is. We are an *energy personality essence* and consist of many essences within many dimensions who seek to speak with you both in words and in the way of spirit. We will say more about this later, but for now, think of us as a *personality gestalt* whose intent is to assist in the ancient ways of teaching.

We refer to our work with Joanne as an *energy exchange*, which is often defined as channeling an essence other than one's own. But this is somewhat of a misnomer because energy exchanges are a natural part of your world. They exist in every capacity: in your atoms, molecules, bodies, and solar systems. Your body was designed to be an energy conductor, so to speak.

Imagine yourself floating in space. The way you know that we provide energy to you sounds simple and it is: trust yourself that you are floating and not falling. The weightless support you feel in floating about the Universe is an exact depiction of how you are intimately connected with God, or All That Is.

You literally float through your days in order to
achieve your intent in life — to be fulfilled — and we

support you energetically. So you can relax and know
that we are always, <u>always</u> here for you.

Your interest in yourself as spirit is reflected by the fact that you chose to read this book. Indeed, you are a wise person for sharing your knowledge with yourself in this manner! We are your wisest selves, so to speak, and since we are inside your consciousness, you have direct access to us *at any time*.

Your intuition is an important tool

The way to access us directly is through your deep intuition, though you may not yet know how to use it. Your intuition was designed to instigate communications from your essence's desires. However, it sometimes gets vetoed by your intellect in the form of wants, which we will discuss a bit later. We are *not* suggesting that your intellect is inferior, for it is also designed to be a very powerful tool. We suggest that you learn to develop your intuition, for it was designed to work harmoniously with your intellect in order to provide you the proper tools to develop your heroic abilities. That's right.

When your intellect and your intuition work together in
harmony, you unleash your own superhero.

We are excited to help you in your superhero quest to dramatically improve your planet and the lives of many individuals. We suggest that you begin immediately, for your planet was in many ways created for this very purpose, and will in many ways not survive without you. We do not exaggerate, as you can see plenty of evidence in your daily news reports. As you learn more about your way of spirit, you will find ways to ensure your planet's safety, for you have the power. So do so.

We will help. We spirits are always here to support you in every way. You only need to ask, then listen with and trust your intuition.

Key Ideas: Introduction

- Rose is an *energy personality essence*—a nonphysical aspect of you—who serves as a teacher.

- Rose engages us through an *energy exchange* with Joanne.

- The term *energy exchange* is often defined as *channeling* an essence other than one's own, but also describes how all things—atoms, molecules, bodies, and solar systems—are intimately connected and supported by All That Is.

- The Seth Material by Jane Roberts and like resources provide valuable information with which to develop your spiritual maturity.

- You are on a heroic journey, with your own intent and purpose. When you become the hero of your own life, you change yourself and your world for the better.

- Learn to trust your intuition. When your intellect and intuition work together, you unleash your own superhero.

Chapter 1: The Way of Spirit

The way of spirit is like a bright, sunny window in which to realize your most fun and fulfilled self. It is as uniquely individual as you would ever hope to find, for the way of spirit is *your* way, not anyone else's.

> *The way of spirit is yours only,*
> *not anyone else's in the world.*

Your wants and desires—which you'll always have—are important things that you'll need to help you discover your way of spirit. There's no reason to believe that your wants and desires ever need to be put aside. They are the keys to help you find your way of spirit, you only need to want and desire the best things for yourself. This book will help you do that, as well as find a balanced and purpose-filled way to be in the world.

The way of spirit is not in any way detrimental to your world, for it never intrudes on the things you desire, or on anyone else's desires. The way of spirit provides not only your greatest fulfillment on a personal level, it increases the fulfillment of your world.

The ideas we suggest in this book might be considered anathema to traditional religious doctrines that say you must deny yourself and "sin no more." Religious doctrines sometimes create the problems that your way of spirit can easily resolve, because it is a soul-affirming—not soul-denying—way. Why would you choose to be physical otherwise?

You chose this physical existence for a purpose

We—the ever-present spirits who accompany you on your life's journey—are always here to assist. For why would spirit exist only outside of your physical world?

Since spirit is in everything, please allow us to help you live more fully in the physical world. We will speak to you any time you wish to hear us, for this was our agreement when you chose to become physical. We will help you to remember this.

Take a moment to listen now through your intuition. Do you hear us?

Again, intuition helps you find your way of spirit, not by itself, but in working together with your logical self. Logic and intuition were created to help you live in your world.

Remember: *you chose this.* You decided before you were born that you would live this physical existence, in this time, in this world.

We want to help you understand—deeply—that the way of spirit is your way, your song, and your desire to remember who you really are!

The individual who is typing these words—Joanne—is an example of someone perfectly suited for her way of spirit, just as you are perfectly suited for yours. The way of spirit draws her to create certain things, including this book. Similar to your own way of spirit, she practices things to assist her in her way of spirit. The essence of Rose whom you will get to know in these pages serves as her own personal spiritual teacher. That's right: the way of spirit intentionally serves *her*, as well as *you*, not the other way around.

You are divine in your own way

The way of spirit is always here to assist you, as well as to help you find the best possible life for yourself. Your way of spirit includes your own Personal God—*your essence*—as well as your own everyday God in flesh—*you!*—for you are divine in your own way. We will explain.

The way you can know your Personal God—your essence—is to make direct contact. This will affect your world in a big way, for when you consider yourself to be anything less than divine, you will find yourselves on the brink of destruction. This was intentional, so as to bring you to your collective senses and allow you to save your planet and yourselves in the process.

Simply look around you. What do you see? You see corruption, toxic environments, pain and suffering. Why? This wasn't how you planned your world to be. Why would you create a way of spirit that includes the suffering of so many individuals?

Because you want to change it. That's right. If you believe that the suffering of your world does not exist in your way of spirit, you are incorrect.

The way of spirit includes all things—joy and
suffering—for you are all things in your world.

This idea will take getting used to. All that you see in your world is a reflection of you that is so intensely personal that you can consider it, in essence, *you.* Your way of spirit is your relationship with your world. Without this larger perspective, your relationship with the world will be a shallow one, for you are *much greater* than you have been raised to believe. You are an expression of essence that includes physical and nonphysical aspects of experience.

Your bliss is in expressing your unique intent

The way of spirit involves finding goodness in your world. Even though there will always be suffering, a person who follows their way of spirit will always strive to help others. This will become clearer in future chapters, so for now, trust that we will help you find ways to reduce suffering in yourself as well as in your world.

All that you need to do to help the world is to try
the best way you know how. In doing so, you'll
find the truest joy you can imagine.

We will help you to discover this in the best, most fulfilling ways possible: finding fun, encouraging others, and enjoying the wealth of spirit. For again, this is the point: when you learn to follow your way of spirit, you will create your best self and the best world possible.

This is not a contradiction. Many of you have been raised to believe that others must suffer if you are to get everything you truly desire. That is a way to say, "Stop doing what makes you happy!" when the opposite is true. The way of spirit will help you to find your bliss, as well as the bliss of all things, at once. Why would it provide anything less? Indeed, the way of spirit is so very interested in your happiness, that it will find *you.*

The way we teach is through words, but the way of spirit for you may be found in any number of wonderful things to know, see, and do. For our purposes, we will sometimes refer to your way of spirit as your *intent.* It extends into spiritual worlds, as well as the physical world when you follow it. It is uniquely, indelibly yours.

That's right: your intent is located in you, always.
The way of spirit is only a matter of finding,
nurturing, and learning to fully express it.

The world needs you! Your spirit helpers are ready and waiting for you to recruit them to help with your everyday challenges as well as your big, wonderful tasks in the world. We want only what you want, so trust that you can learn to easily communicate with your own spirit helpers.

We're a fun bunch, not stuffy like you have been taught to believe. We want to assist, for what else, indeed, would there be to do but sit around on clouds filing our spirit nails? That's right: nothing. So trust that we're ready as well as able to assist.

Now, we want to assure you that *the* way of spirit, in the general sense, is not *your* way of spirit in the individual sense. By this we mean that you need to tailor the way of spirit to your own needs. This will require you to deeply consider the meaning of the words we use.

Don't try to follow your way of spirit because "Rose said so," or that anyone "said so." Be discerning with everything you read. Don't parrot our words, *use* them. Your religious upbringing has been, in some ways, deeply shallow. We are joking, of course, but this is the point: you need to find your way of spirit in the *deepest* sense possible.

We essences are always watching. Every hair on your head, every beautiful loving way you express yourself, every inch of skin on your body, is important to us. We love you and want your greatest fulfillment.

So trust that we'll be watching, to help you find your best expressions, and to tell you when you're doing things that help you be the most fulfilled self you can be.

In us, you have your own cheerleading section, on Cloud Nine.

Do you hear us?

Key Ideas: The Way of Spirit

- The way of spirit is uniquely yours, not anyone else's. It is your innate *intent* that you can learn to find, nurture, and fully express.
- Your wants and desires are the keys to finding your way of spirit.
- The way of spirit serves you, not the other way around. It provides your greatest fulfillment on a personal and collective level. You can't have one without the other.
- All that you see in your world is a reflection of you that is so intensely personal that you can consider it, in essence, *you*. Your way of spirit is your relationship with your world.
- Your way of spirit contains all things—joy and suffering.
- You are an expression of essence that includes physical and nonphysical aspects of experience.
- Be discerning, and remember essence will always assist.

Chapter 2: You Live in Exciting Times

We will tell you a short story to help you understand how we spirits work, and we mean *work*. For you've been raised to believe that work is bad, but it is wonderful when your work is interesting and fun.

Many individuals in your world should receive a bonus, for their work is so frequently tedious and painful. To correct this would be a good first step in changing your world for the better. And you can begin by first providing yourself with the work you love.

When you pursue the work you love,
you follow your way of spirit.

This sounds simple, and it will be once you determine what that is. It is also the greatest way to transform your world, for if your world is to be populated with only individuals who enjoy their work, there would be far less suffering, greater compassion, and better lives for all creatures of the world. This is the point of finding your bliss, for in doing so, you do your God's work in the world.

That's simple, right? That's right, for your bliss is what you've been hard-wired to have. So when you learn to follow your bliss in terms of work that supports you, the way of spirit will move you into areas of ever deeper fulfillment and help you find how your particular way of spirit will work in the world.

How you feel inside is how you see the world

The way of spirit is, as we've said, different for everyone. The following story will give you a brief overview to help you understand the way of spirit, and how you might find your bliss.

Once upon a time there was a boy and a girl who wanted to be happy. They looked and looked for ways to be happy, but only found ways to be sad. This was because they only looked *outside* themselves to find what they would call true love, true wealth, and true happiness. In this, they found a great many things, but always wanted more. For this was what they found—*things*—and they could never get enough things to be truly happy.

They didn't like, or notice much, that the world provided them with clean air, clean water, and clean spiritual beliefs. They believed that the world was dirty, and ugly, and unsafe. They did things—such as work in jobs they did not love, act in ways they did not enjoy, and have interests in things that did not assist them—to get what they wanted. But what they wanted was never what the world provided.

One day, they discovered that they were in the world. That's right. *They didn't notice before that they were in the world.* They had been fooling themselves into *thinking* they were in the world, but they were not. And the place they thought of as the world was exactly the way they felt inside—dirty, ugly, and unsafe.

When they stopped thinking about what a horrible place the world was, they realized that the world was not at all what they *thought*. They noticed that the world was a beautiful, often surprising place full of sensory experiences—images, tastes, sounds, smells, and feelings.

They suddenly understood that they were being provided a world that was there to meet all their needs, and it was. They also discovered that the world was not there to make them happy in ways they had expected, but to make them happy in ways they didn't expect.

They felt so much better, not being wound up so tightly in their unreasonable expectations. They noticed how others were wound up in their unreasonable expectations, too, some so tightly that they finally just wound up and died. That's right. They just died inside. And they found—as you can, too—a million people who have died inside. And that is exactly what you are dealing with: the living dead.

This story is easily interpreted. What do you feel like inside? Do you see the connection between how you feel inside with how you see the world? Do you find satisfaction in your days? Do you find satisfaction in your nights? Do you see how important this is?

You're right to find satisfaction in your days *and* nights, and this includes your sexual activities. If you're not, you should be, for if you turn off your sense of *senxuality*—the combination of both sexual and sensual sense—you deprive yourself of your deepest connection with spirit. That's right: your way of spirit is in your senxuality.

The way of spirit is in your most gratified self, and you'd do well to embrace your sense of divine senxuality, for your senxuality is your God-given gift, and you would be incorrect to cut off your sense of Divinity by considering this glorious aspect of your physical nature sinful.

Your way of spirit includes your Godlike self

Now, you'll notice this chapter is titled "You Live in Exciting Times." That's why we wanted to tell you a bit about your senxuality: it is an important way to make your life more fulfilling. Don't expect that your way of spirit will be devoid of your senxuality, it won't. Trust that your way of spirit will satisfy you in every way—and we mean *every* way—in your bodies, minds, and spirits.

Again, your wants and desires are important in helping you discover your way of spirit. The way of spirit will help you get your desires met in ways you've never dreamed of, or even expect.

For example, you may want a boat, but if the boat is not in alignment with your way of spirit, you won't get your boat. Do you say, "That's okay, maybe the boat isn't for me"? That would be a good thing, because you would consider alternatives that you hadn't before. Do you want a boat in ways that would support your way of spirit? We suggest not, because if it did, you would have your boat. The way of spirit allows your boat to come to you, or not. Now, did you say, "We need that boat, and by God we will get that boat!"? Not if you were following your way of spirit.

The way of spirit allows you to think in different terms than perhaps you do now, because it involves <u>all</u> of you, not just your ego self.

Your ego is considered a fine thing in many ways, even by us spirits, but your ego self doesn't call the shots in every way, no matter what it tells you. So trust that when your ego says it wants something, your greater self may not, and the greater self always gets what it desires. *Always!* That's right, for your greater self is your God, and your God is you. So you can think of yourself as a God or Goddess, but only in certain ways.

We will excuse you for a moment while you mull this over, for you need to really comprehend this.

We will wait. That's right. We're waiting for you to consider that you are Gods before we continue.

Now, you may sometimes think of yourself as Gods, but this will not always be accurate, for your ego is not God, God is God, and your ego is a *part* of God.

We will say more about this later, but for now, just think of yourself for a moment as God. What would you do? Would you strive to make your world better? Would you correct someone for something they did that was incorrect? We say: *yes you would.* So why would you not act in a Godly way? Why would you not set your expectations of being God in ways that would be Godlike? Because you're afraid to.

The way to get past your fear is to allow yourself the notion that your ego is not in charge. If your ego was in charge, it would wreak havoc, and God doesn't do that.

You can speak with your Personal God

The way to find out what kind of God you are is to speak with your essence, your Personal God. In this, we will assist. Wanting to find your Personal God is the first step, and is the most wonderful thing you can do. You've been taught that you need to go through someone else—such as a priest—to access God. This is the most preposterous thing that you could have been taught, as well as the most damaging.

In fact, your God wants desperately to speak with you, and shall, for you have the ability. That's right: *you!* So trust that you *can* speak with your God in ways that you will find truly, beautifully intimate, as well as understandable, for your God understands you better than anyone in your world could. For your God is like Rose, only yours and yours alone.

Would your God speak to you like Rose would? Yes and no. While Rose is Godlike in the sense that she is a collection of divine essences, she's only helping you to find *your* God. So Rose can be considered a mediator and helper. The important thing is that you find *your* God, for your God is *your God* in every way. In your way of spirit, he or she will assist in ways that Rose cannot, for your God is intentionally designed to provide you with the very best life possible. In this your God is interested, and that is all. *That's all!*

All your God wants is to help you, nothing more.

In this, you can relax your expectations that you're in the world to serve your God. While this is correct in some ways, the God you serve is *your* Personal God—not anyone else's—and you can trust that your God will not make unfair demands on you. Your God knows what you need better than anyone, even you.

So while you may sometimes have conflict in finding or following your way of spirit, your God knows that's what you came into physical reality to do. Whenever you fear that your way of spirit seems untrue or wrong, this is only your ego speaking.

Your ego sometimes wants things that you've been convinced you should have, and your ego expects you to find a way past your fears to get what it thinks you want in order for you to be satisfied. But in the long run, your *ego* will not get what it wants, but your *God* will, and your God is *you*: your essence self.

So you can trust yourself to be your God in ways that you will find fully satisfying, even through your roughest spots, for these will hold keys to your own satisfying life. We will say more about the rough spots later, and for now, will leave you with your Personal God to assist with understanding why this is the most exciting time to be alive. Why?

We will allow you a moment to get your own answers.

That's right. That's right. That's right.

This is the most exciting time to be alive because you're waking up to your Gods and your own beautiful expressions of Godhood in ways that will blossom all over the world.

In this, you need only to learn to follow your way of spirit.

That's right! That's right! That's right!

Key Ideas: You Live in Exciting Times

- Your way of spirit includes finding work you love.
- The world is here to meet all your needs and make you happy in ways you don't always want or expect.
- Your *senxual*—sexual and sensual—nature is a divine gift, and a way to connect deeply with spirit.
- The way of spirit involves *all* of you, including your essence self, not just your ego self.
- You can speak with your Personal God—your essence—in ways that you will find beautifully intimate and understandable, for your God understands you better than anyone, and wants to help.
- This is the most exciting time to be alive because you're waking up to your Gods and expressions of Godhood.

Chapter 3: Your Amazing Contrary Self

Your way of spirit sometimes includes things you'll find quite challenging, for you're so conditioned to expect certain things, and fear certain things, that you'd do well to forget everything you've learned about how life should be.

This may sound terrible, but ask yourself: "Is my life so perfect that I'd do well to <u>not</u> learn something totally new?" If the answer is yes, then you're probably already following your way of spirit, and won't need to avail yourself of this book. But if you think that you'd do well to change—and we do mean *change*—then we suggest you read on, for change is what you'll need to be truly happy, and this sometimes isn't easy.

To decide, you'll need to consider another very important question, not just "Do I *want to* change?" but "*Can* I change?"

Trust that you *can* change, as well as find your fearlessness, for once you have a bit of your way of spirit in you, there will be no stopping you. For the way of spirit invests in *you*, too, in ways that will power you through all your days and beyond.

The way of spirit will never leave you
once you decide to live it.

Let's explore what you need to do to find your way of spirit, which will be easier when you consider that the way of spirit wants to find *you*, too.

Your contrary self is an aspect of your Personal God

What's the best way to begin? The way of spirit will find you in surprising ways, in ways you wouldn't think of on your worst day, and then some. For your way of spirit will find you in ways that seem funny—and perhaps even tragic—when you least expect it. That's when the way of spirit is at its best: when you're at your worst. When this occurs, you can trust that the way of spirit has found you, and it does so in ways that you'll find contrary.

You'll find your sense of contrariness to be the most important tool you can have, as well as friend, for there is no better friend than your *contrary self—an aspect of your essence self that loves you exactly as you are, no matter what.* The way you will know this is easy: doesn't your very best friend tell you exactly what you *don't want* to hear, but really *need* to hear sometimes? That's right.

> *Your contrary self tells you what you need to know,*
> *in spite of the fact that your ego will many times not*
> *want to hear it or take action.*

In this respect, the whole Universe will conspire to shake you out of your ways that oppose it and thrust you into the ways that you *truly need*—that you *desire*—to embrace. For your contrary self is indeed that voice inside your head that says, "We want you to do things differently." And your ego self will say either "Okay!" or "No way!"

This is something important to think about when you begin to follow your way of spirit, for it may be indicated by your contrary self in ways you may initially find terrible. But that's *exactly* the way to tell yourself what you need to look into, for in time, you'll find the contrary self indeed knows best.

> *Your contrary self is the best means of*
> *communication with your Personal God.*

You can trust we know what we're talking about, for we've done so many things to help individuals see things in ways they wouldn't normally, that you'd find them funny until they happen to you.

We're talking about hurricanes, zits, interesting ways of expressing oneself like farting loudly on *American Idol*, and getting sick when you wouldn't normally want that, not that you ever would. But although illness or bodily misfortune has its own purpose, there will be times that you'll find it to be most embarrassing—like bleeding on someone, or vomiting on your beautiful blouse, or someone else's, and myriad other things that you'd find to be the most embarrassing in the world. And that's exactly the point: the contrary self wants to get your attention.

The way of spirit is at times a most contrary way to discover the path to find your best life possible. And you'll find, as we've said, that this is sometimes the most embarrassing or unfathomably uncomfortable thing you could imagine. And why wouldn't it be?

Why else would you create challenging situations if you weren't trying to find ways to get your own attention? Because you've decided that life is supposed to be a series of comfortable ways that inspire only beautiful things—not gassy ways, not slovenly bleeding-all-over-everyone ways— but ways that should always be pretty and pristine. This is not life! This is a fairy tale that you've bought into that helps you *manage* — rather than *live* — your life and that no longer serves you. In reality, the way of spirit sometimes feels unfitting, uncomfortable, and unbending. Indeed, your way of spirit is fitting for you: you just haven't found *how* yet.

Your contrary self will help you on your path

The way of spirit will move you in ways that you will find most contrary, as well as painful, at times, but you'd do well to listen to your contrary self. How can you find it? As we said, your contrary self is your finest friend who will guide you toward the best, most wonderful expressions. For your contrary self will proudly speak up in any situation when it feels left out.

That's correct: your contrary self sends messages to you and to the world that may seem unpopular, wrongheaded, as well as fun... as well as glamorous and popular... *not!*

> *Your contrary self is not interested in winning beauty or popularity contests: your contrary self is only interested in your happiness.*

Why would you believe that you're most happy when you're popular? Indeed, isn't this a break in your thinking already? We suggest you first tell your friends that you don't want their approval, and then say that to the rest of the world, for your popularity is perhaps the least important thing in your world. Indeed, *your works — your creative expressions guided by loving kindness* — are the most important things in your world.

The contrary self is sometimes like a snarling shepherd dog that herds a flock of sheep into submission. The sheep don't want the dog around. They want only to spryly play and graze in their field, and ignore the reality of dangerous situations from which they need to be shepherded toward safety. The sheep would stray into the jaws of another creature if they were allowed to guard themselves. Why don't they want the dog around? Because the dog is contrary. That's the point!

> *The contrary self shepherds you in ways that may annoy you at first, because it will not allow you to stray off your path.*

Left alone, your sheep self will find ways to drop off cliffs. But your contrary shepherd dog self will bark to get you on your way of spirit, and bite you in the butt when you need it.

So take heed! The way of spirit, as we've said, is sometimes treacherous. So you'll do well to learn to recognize your contrary self, for it is a she-bitch who will guard you with her very life, and that, indeed, is a most beautiful thing.

Indeed, why would you not trust the she-bitch contrary self? Why wouldn't you want the way of spirit to capture your attention in this way? It is because you don't feel that it's important enough to deserve such a wonderful action. But it is, and *your contrary she-bitch self wants only your happiness.*

Trust the voice of your contrary self

The contrary self is your most wonderful friend in the world, as well as *funny.* She is so very interested in assisting you that you'll find her to be in your head at times when you least expect it.

For instance, say you want to try to water ski. The contrary self says, "We will assist." Then, as you wait on the dock, your contrary self says, "You know, I don't think this is a good idea after all. Why don't you just sit this one out?" Then you say to the she-bitch, "Why didn't you tell me this before I put on the skis? Why didn't you tell me this before I got to the pier, waiting to take off in my beautiful bathing suit?"

And your contrary self will say, "That's fine. Just make sure your bathing suit is on tightly." In this way, the contrary self will make you laugh, indeed, and that's what it's for.

So you can find that she's always willing to be the buffoon as well as the most loving friend you can have. For why would the way of spirit provide you anything less? It won't. And in this, you'll learn to lighten up your attitude so much that you won't need water skis to make waves on top of the water, for you'll walk on it.

Indeed, isn't the way of spirit like walking on water? How do you think that Wonderful Fellow did it if he didn't allow his sometimes nagging contrary self to tell him to lighten up? Indeed, he couldn't. The contrary self will allow you a lightness of being that will help you in every way. For why would you want to go through life in such a sad state of seriousness? Indeed, you don't. So trust your contrary self to help you laugh at yourself in ways that you'll find truly helpful.

*Trust that when the little contrary voice of your
Personal God tells you what to do,
that you'll want to listen.*

Indeed, she'll be so happy to be heard that she won't believe it. For your contrary self has been so incredibly stifled that it will find ways to wonderfully amuse you just so that you continue to listen, as, indeed, she's been created to do.

The way to allow the contrary self more ability to reach you is through the Access Alternatives practice.[1] The practice will help you get out of closed patterns of thinking by providing different ideas and perspectives for past or current situations or decisions that you may not otherwise consider. The contrary views will help you choose most wisely when viewing any situation, and are an extremely important part of owning and living your life, rather than coasting along in ways that only manage it and don't bring you fulfillment.

The contrary self is incredibly important for your world, as well as your way of spirit. We will explore this further in later chapters. For now, just remember that your contrary self, when sufficiently stifled, will not be able to help you out of destructive choices and behaviors.

Next, we will explore additional ways to find your way of spirit, and how your contrary self will tell you exactly what you need to do to be happy and beautifully create your wonderful life.

Key Ideas: Your Amazing Contrary Self

- Trust that you can make changes in your life, and that you will find fearlessness.
- There is no better friend than your *contrary self*, an aspect of your essence self that tells you what you need to know in spite of the fact that your ego may not want to hear it or take action.
- Life is not supposed to be comfortable and pristine. This belief will only allow you to manage—rather than live— your life, and no longer serves you.

---

[1] See the Access Alternatives practice on page 187.

- Your works—creative expressions guided by loving kindness—are the most important things to accomplish in your world, not your popularity.
- If you don't pay attention, you can stifle or override your contrary self, who is there to help you avoid destructive choices and behaviors.

Chapter 4: The Families of Intent

An important way to discover your way of spirit is to determine your superhero ways. As we said earlier, you were born with the same sort of heroic abilities as any superhero, though you may have yet to identify them. Indeed, there are an infinite number of ways to explore these superpowers, but you need some guidelines to help you.

We'll introduce these in ways that may sound concrete at first, but they are not. These heroic qualities are presented as guidelines only. They are not a means to fit you into certain categories, but a means to explore various *characteristics within your consciousness* right now.

We call these superhero qualities the *families of intent*. They work together to create your physical universe, which you, as well as your expressions, are an important part of.

There are nine families of intent. Why nine? Why *not* nine? As we suggested, these are only guidelines for you to find your own heroic qualities that will help you define personal *ease areas* as well as *challenge areas*.

We will say more about this later. In the meantime, think of your way of spirit as including *all* of your families of intent in different degrees, starting with the ones you'll favor most. In this, you'll find them, and they'll find you.

The families of intent are part your spiritual heritage

The families of intent have been offered by Seth[2] and other spiritual teachers throughout history. Sometimes they are referred to in angelic terms, other times in psychological terms, but they are the same, just clothed differently depending on the times they inhabit. The way you'll know that these are accurate is not because a bunch of ghosts said they were, but because you know deeply in your essence that they are.

The vast majority of physical realities incorporate these same families of intent. In this, you can think of your essence as a multidimensional being who pursues experiences in many different times and dimensions, and when it pursues experiences in physical dimensions, it explores these general creative themes in infinite ways.

The families of intent, along with their associated colors (to help you identify them in your dreams and intuitions)[3], are:

Name	Pronunciation	Intent	Color
Sumafi	Su-MA-fee	Teachers	Grey/Black
Sumari	Su-MAR-ee	Artists	Blue
Ilda	IL-da	Exchangers	Green
Gramada	Gra-MA-da	Formers	Orange
Vold	Vold	Reformers	Yellow
Tumold	TU-mold	Healers	Indigo
Zuli	ZU-lee	Imagers	Purple
Milumet	MIL-you-may	Rememberers	Red
Borledim	BOR-le-dim	Nurturers	Pink

---

[2] Seth's version is provided in *The Unknown Reality: Volume Two* by Jane Roberts (Amber-Allen Publishing, Inc., 1996), pp. 581–600.

[3] Elias provided the *belonging-to* and *aligning-with* designations and associated colors. For more information, visit eliasforum.org.

Sumafi (Teachers)

The Sumafi are most interested in the least distorted teachings that you can imagine. *The Way of Spirit* is a work of your Sumafi family, as Rose is a Sumafi essence who wishes to "learn" you well. We made a joke, but you can see that we want to make things clear as well as accurate, for your civilization has been fraught with highly distorted teachings for many years.

In this, the Sumafi do not teach *the* way of spirit—in the sense of a *general* way of spirit—for *all*. They do not attempt to ban or destroy distorted teachings, for these are not incorrect in the sense they are what you want, or have wanted in the past, for your own experience. However, the Sumafi do want to make sure that authentic information is maintained and passed on.

The ways of your Sumafi hold many truths, but
in many respects there are no truths, only beliefs.
In this, you'll find that truths are those beliefs
that you find truthful.

So the Sumafi will find ways to inculcate in your world the truest form of spiritual ideas, not "The" Truth. The only Truth—with a capital "T"—is the Truth of Yourself.

In this, you will find the beautiful expression of Truth in your life, should you want that, indeed. For your truest expressions are those that fill your heart with the authenticity that you feel inside and validate through your own direct experience, not through what others tell you.

So embrace your Sumafi intent to discover your truest expressions, and you will always find the Truth within you.

Sumari (Artists)

The Sumari create works of art that speak the ancient truths needed for your civilization to flower. Artistic endeavors are not limited only to the Sumari, but they have an intent that is focused on making the world better through spiritually informed works.

The Sumari long for better worlds and better ways of life. They sometimes make great strides in social change through their artistic works. They find ways to use the arts to change minds, change ways, and change politics. They always seek to make their way of spirit as artful as possible.

In this, they may interest themselves in many forms of artistic endeavor, and find new and unique ways to create works that may not be considered artistic but *will* be artistic in the hands of Sumari individuals. They want to change your world in ways that are beautiful and spiritual in the aesthetic rather than religious sense, although they will sometimes create artistic works of religion as well.

Sumari take on many forms of expression that you'll find obvious and not so obvious.

They work in ways that defy your arts as you define them, and reshape the arts in ways you wouldn't recognize, because their way is to change how you look at the world.

In this, the Sumari are sometimes persecuted and temporarily excluded from your mainstream. For this reason, Sumari tend not to be born into timeframes that impede the creation of artistic works, such as your Dark Ages. They thrive in your current timeframe as you collectively move into areas that allow them greater ease of creativity and usefulness in ways that you'll find truly groundbreaking.

We trust you'll find many Sumari individuals who love the times you live in now, so go for it Sumari! We want to take your art home in literal ways, as well as soulful ways, for in your artistry you'll help all individuals sense in themselves *their* deepest, most thrilling ways of artistry and new ways to assert themselves as spiritual creatures in your world.

Ilda (Exchangers)

The Ilda are exchangers of many things: ideas, impressions, languages, artworks, sciences, philosophies, and ideologies that help cultures change in helpful ways. For example, they help change geographies, money markets, and the ways of sex, as many of your Ilda are the best courtesans who enjoy crossing cultural boundaries.

In this, the Ilda excel in your lifetime
because they find ways to "connect the dots"
between different cultures.

The reason the Berlin Wall fell had much to do with the remnants of sovereignty that the Ilda were compelled to tear down in ways that were less about tearing and more about sharing cultural exchanges. The wall, therefore, was intrinsically symbolic of the Ilda stature, in a sense, rather than the stature of kingdoms. The action that transpired was a most grand connection of the dots that allowed healing of a part of the world long ravaged by divisions of geography, politics, and social and economic structures.

Ilda are also your jesters and comedians, whom we are quite fond of, and will be very important in the coming years.

You need your Ilda to make jokes, to make fun of your social institutions, and to exchange ideas in ways that you'll find breathtaking, especially given the growth of your global networks, which are an Ilda creation in many respects.

Global connectivity provides many new opportunities for Ilda, because they'll find ways to cross various boundaries that engage your imaginations in amusing and spiritually oriented ways. You need your Ilda to break down your walls with good natured humor as well as rivalry that promotes healthy change.

Gramada (Formers)

The Gramada often take whatever is at hand and make something spectacular that hasn't been invented before.

The Gramada often conclude things by starting things, and in starting things, conclude things. In other words, they're formers as well as un-formers, for their formation of things new or improved start and end things, and make great strides in your world in astonishing ways. While you do indeed create your own reality, it is in many ways formed by your Formers essence selves.

They hold a great many patents as well. When you find something new that seems so incredibly useful and you wonder how you ever got along without it, your Formers were involved in most beautiful ways.

In some respects, you could call your Gramada inventors, but the better terms would be synthesizers or improvisers, as they improvise things that at first may seem jauntily improbable. In this, they synthesize many ideas—old and new—in ways that haven't been realized before so that you may best enjoy your earthly experiences.

The Gramada have a knack for potentiating things that allow for the diversity in others. They may find that in order to get to where the world wants to be, they must include a vast array of different ideas as well as talents. So in their way of spirit, they may form whole companies, or nations, to ensure the intent of the Formers family is incorporated into your world.

Your Gramada selves will continue to form amazing, helpful things in your lifetime, including a time machine. Indeed, we are peeking into the future, but that's only in terms of what we perceive as your most probable futures.

> *If there's a way to create a time machine —*
> *and indeed there is, as you know that*
> *anything is possible — it will be your*
> *Gramada who will do so.*

We look forward to seeing your Gramada take flight in ways they will find most wonderful, and so will you!

Vold (Reformers)

The Vold are formers, too, in the sense that their goal is to reshape things in ways that need it. However, their forming often occurs in revolutionary ways that provoke change.

> *In their quest for reform, they will find*
> *any contrary and subtle way to shake*
> *things up, for your Vold seek to reform*
> *your collective ways.*

You'll find the Vold out on your picket lines calling for social changes, instigating political coups, as well as finding peaceful ways of change. Indeed, the Vold need to change in peaceful rather than violent ways, for why would you want more violence in your world?

So the Vold have important missions to provide—as well as peaceful ones—and will need mature and sound ideas to provide change so that ruling parties who require change won't know what hit them. Indeed, there are many ways to influence change as well as revolution that aren't violent, so the Vold need to explore their ways of spirit to find the answers to create provocatively beautiful things as well as constructive results.

The Vold have strong interactions with all the other families of intent, as every product of any family requires the various talents of each. All of your families of intent need the revolutionary Vold ways in their ways of spirit.

What would you get when you merge Vold Reformers with Ilda Exchangers, for example? You'd get incredible new ways to exchange information that you'd consider revolutionary, such as the Internet or a way to share music online that is fair to all parties and allows music to reach many. What would you get when you merge Vold Reformers with Gramada Formers? We'll say that you'd get something out of this world. The time travel machine we mentioned when speaking about Gramada is a perfect example. What you would do with time travel would change your world in revolutionary ways.

We suggest you consider all of the ramifications of this kind of "cross breeding" and discover your own powers of reform when you reach inside yourself, as well as connect with other individuals who carry the Vold intent, for they'll help you to start and sustain the revolution of ideas so desperately needed in your world.

Tumold (Healers)

The Tumold heal in ways that might surprise you, because they facilitate your own healing energies. The way they facilitate is the key, but it is not the expression you may normally think of as healing.

Those of Tumold intent would do well to understand their way of spirit most. The planet and its occupants are in such desperate need of physical, emotional, mental, and spiritual healing that they'd be overwhelmed should their way of spirit be limited to the "saving" ways of healing done in your current medical professions. The Tumold way of spirit says, "Healer, heal yourself before attempting to heal anyone else."

Tumold intent doesn't actually heal others, it facilitates individual healing in miraculous ways, for all of your health issues—your physical, emotional, and mental issues—are related to spiritual issues as well.

Spiritual healing is therefore important, as are the many ways that spirit heals through applications such as vitamins, minerals, reiki, and acupuncture. But they all have at least a little—sometimes a lot—to do with spiritual things, as well as mental, emotional, and bodily things. So your Tumold must facilitate their own spiritual health before they can assist in the proactive healing of others.

The Tumold will have methods so diverse that they will divide the medical establishment who want to provide one-size-fits-all cures for dis-ease. Their methods will seem strange to some, and will include methods such as meditation, musical instruction to help guide your inner experiences in healing ways, and other methods to help you remember your inner healing abilities.

The Tumold may wish to avoid the medical establishment in some ways, but not altogether, for it does get things right sometimes and finds miraculous cures. Your current medical establishment practices do follow some ways of spirit. For instance, the practices that involve relief from pain are based on practical, plant energy-based remedies that still have value in medical environments.

So trust that you'll need to discover only your way of health, and not anyone else's. The Tumold intent will do so, and holds the promise of wonderful healing ways.

Zuli (Imagers)

The Zuli excel in the creation of all bodily forms: people, beasts, commercial buildings, cars, as well as expressions of sportsmanship, dance, and other physical feats you consider miraculous.

The Imagers will play an important role in your future in a variety of ways, because they will assist in the formation of a new breed of individual.

The Zuli explore all physical forms in ways that inspire. Though they have a wonderful way of spirit, they will need to find new ways to correct the imbalances of your world. These imbalances have to do with extraordinary feats of form that need new inspiration in ways that are spiritually sound. For why would you design a building that crumbles so easily in an earthquake, or trap individuals in them as they fall because their staircases are too high when the elevators fail? The Imagers need to humanize forms in new ways, so trust them to create new forms that will be sound as well as beautiful.

The Zuli sometimes insist that their best pleasures are found in things, and they will discover that the purely material aspects of life may not be the most fulfilling. They will at times need to reconsider what their strengths truly are, so as to create the best forms in your world. Does the best concoction of steroids truly express physical excellence by virtue of achieving the best batting records in baseball? The Imagers will set the bar in ways that allow those who wish to potentiate their best forms of bodily expression without relying on artificial means to attain physical excellence.

So the Zuli will find exceptional ways of spirit to realize the most beautiful human forms, but not necessarily in the ways they've followed to date. For they need to encourage beauty in *outward* ways, yes, but in doing so must reach *inside* individuals so as to find the more subtle ways of imaging yourselves.

The Zuli also find great benefits in the area of sexual activity. Though sex is often considered a physical expression, this is not its truest form. Imagers' sexual ways will need to look into peoples' souls as well as their bodies to provide the truest form of union in spiritual terms.

When the Zuli fully embrace their way of spirit, they will recreate your images as Gods- and Goddesses-in-flesh, for their way of spirit promotes just that!

Milumet (Rememberers)

The Milumet make a very wide mark in your world, but their ways are so discreet that you need to pay very close attention in order to see what they're up to. The Milumet are so in tune with your natural order and reveal themselves in ways so subtly beautiful that you sometimes don't recognize it. For the Milumet remember what you have forgotten.

They hold the *remembrance* of your essence nature—*your soul nature*—that many of you have lost touch with. They can help in extraordinary ways, for they incorporate *natural time* that exists *beyond* clock time and is in tempo with the earth's natural rhythms. Their natural time sense makes Milumet intent extraordinary, for they are able to participate in the world in ways that are devoutly secure in their knowledge of self.

In this, they may sometimes be considered simple or naïve, but this is not the case: they are smarter than anyone, in some ways. They may only look naïve, but this is the trick of Milumet. They know what you need in ways you don't, for they're the keepers of knowledge, the keepers of wisdom, the keepers of natural things that bring life to your planet.

The Milumet way of spirit is of the utmost importance today because it's needed to assist in the protection of your earth, your animals, your air, and other things that are so very important that you constantly forget about them. That's okay, because your Milumet remember, and you will remember when you embrace your Milumet selves as well.

The Milumet hold the awareness to allow you the best memory of your world in order to restore yourselves as well as your planet in ways that will be whole again.

They remember the ways of spirit that will hold the promise of tomorrow. They will also become the most engaging way of spirit for many, since their ways are so very simple so as to be the most attractive.

Borledim (Nurturers)

The Borledim assist in your ways of spirit that involve children. Indeed, your children are among the most neglected creatures on your planet, and they also hold the promise of tomorrow. Why would you not pay close attention to them?

*The Borledim way of spirit calls on you to
allow compassion for your children as well
as creatures in your world.*

They are the ones who reach out to help more than any of the other family intents. They also assist the adults of your world to bring harmony and health to your planet. For what more is an adult than a child grown up?

Indeed, many adults are miserable because they no longer improvise in childlike ways. They often deliberately dissuade children from their play and make them miserable as well. So trust your Borledim to assist not just your adults who need to be reminded of their inner child, but to nurture your children as well.

The Borledim allow only the healthiest forms of expression in children as well as adults who at times don't know better. We suggest that too many adults act like children and need to be reminded of their manners. We suggest you need to redefine the word "nurture" so as to promote responsibility in individuals who need to be told "no" at times. In this, the Borledim are often great facilitators of teams and organizations because they help bring out the best in individuals and provide a sense of guided nurturing that promotes teamwork and positive, effective results.

The Borledim also need to adjust your ways of nurturing others in ways that help the *truly* underprivileged and underserved children and creatures in your world. Trust your Borledim to cut off the great wealth to those who only look after themselves and get help to those who deserve it. We trust this may sound stern, but why would you continue to respond so unhealthily to individuals who only care about themselves? Your entire social system could collapse if you continue this, so allow your Borledim intent to do its work to nurture your world. We trust you will!

Your essence expresses intent in infinite ways

Next, we will explore how these innate intents function in yourself and your life. The life you lead now is only one of many, and your way of spirit influences all your lifetimes in astonishing ways.

The way of spirit, as we've said, includes that of your essence. Your essence has many lifetimes in this and other dimensions that are quite different from this one. Your essence has many ways of knowing things, and acquires a great wealth of information from these lifetimes that consist of many different forms, dimensions, and timeframes. The multidimensional wonders that your essence knows is—as you can imagine—*vast!* The knowledge is *always* available to you, so as to assist in your daily life. And in this, your essence wants to assist.

Your essence *belongs to* a family of intent that is your innate intent *in every lifetime*. It is a theme that colors all of your lifetimes. Which of the nine families of intent do you intuitively connect with? Which of them do you feel may have helped to guide you on your way of spirit thus far? This can be considered your *ease area* since your essence is so very familiar with this family of intent.

You *align with* a family of intent that is your *intent in this lifetime*. It is a *challenge area* that allows you to investigate various families' unique expressions and help you develop your abilities to their fullest. In this, you'll find a natural aptitude, but it will often have challenges built in.

You can trust your essence—no matter what—to always have your best interests in mind. When you, as essence, choose to have a physical lifetime, you do so with specific intentions of having certain types of experiences. Your experiences inform your essence in ways that inform individuals in other lifetimes that you, as essence, have. Since space and time are constructs of physical reality, you can more accurately consider lifetimes as *focuses of attention* that essence has *simultaneously*. In this, your essence is a most mighty, wonderful being, and you would do well to get to know it better.

We will repeat that.

You would do well to get to know your essence in a big way, as its main job is to <u>always</u> love and support you.

Again, your essence is your Personal God—a vast, multidimensional being that you can think of as "One-Made-of-Many." For indeed, you are your very own *Youniverse* and as such, don't need to ever think of yourself as alone again. Isn't that wonderful?

Trust yourself to find which family of intent is in alignment with your deepest desires, as well as the things that interest you most, for they will lead you to your way of spirit.

The most important thing you can do is to discover and do what you're most passionate about! This is the key to living a beautiful and fulfilling life.

Identifying your family of intent belonging-to and aligning-with areas, and an intent name to help define your works in the world, are powerful tools to help you on your way of spirit. While your essence is nameless, you can give it a name to help you most deeply identify and tune into your vast, multidimensional nature, your Youniverse.[4]

Don't take our word for it: find out for yourself! And as you do, be assured that your way of spirit will find you too!

Key Ideas: The Families of Intent

- The nine families of intent are characteristics of consciousness that work together to create this physical universe and many others.

- Your essence *belongs to* one or more family. This *belonging-to* intent colors every lifetime that you live. It can be considered an *ease area* in which your reality creation is effortless.

- Your current lifetime is one of many *focuses of attention* your essence lives. Each focus *aligns with* one or more of the nine families. Your *aligning-with* can be considered a *challenge area* through which you experience the benefits and shortcomings of that creative theme in everyday life.

- Identifying your essence's belonging-to and lifetime aligning-with, your intent name, and your *essence name*, will help you discover and do what you're most passionate about. This is the key to living a beautiful and fulfilling life—your way of spirit. (See the Intent Practices on page 189.)

---

[4] See the Intent Practices on page 189.

Chapter 5: The Way of Spirit
Will Find You

The way of spirit wants to find you, to allow your very best expressions of selfhood and create the best life for yourself. To do so, your essence is always ready to assist in your desires, but not in all of your wants, for your desires are natural impulses coming from your essence. Your wants, as we said, will get in the way of finding your best expressions when they are not in harmony with your desires. In this way, your wants will sometimes be healthy and satisfying, and sometimes will not be. You can think of desires as wants that are the healthiest expressions of your selfhood.

The way you'll find your way of spirit is in your desires, nothing more, nothing less.

You can trust that when you get truly excited
and passionate about something, you're
following your way of spirit.

Wants can *be*—and *become*—passions and desires

We use the term *passion* to identify *what gets you excited in a spiritual sense,* because your essence is always present to intuitively nudge you to realize your desires. Sometimes it will involve other individuals, so you can relax. We are not telling you to avoid sexual union, although you might do well to consider yourselves in deeper unions than you may have availed yourselves of at present.

So, of course, passionate desires can apply to people, but there are also ideas and things in your world that you may desire in a very big way. These are another important part of your way of spirit. Simple, isn't it? Indeed, why wouldn't it be? For your way of spirit sings from the depths of your heart every day.

As you learn to heed the siren call of your desires,
you will determine the authentic course of your life
and follow your way of spirit.

Now, you often interest yourself in wants that many other individuals share. For instance, you want effective governments. Most wants start out as excellent ways to spur passion as well as creativity, but old wants often become dull. You would do well to continue to pursue your more effective wants—such as peace, love, and understanding—but you may sometimes need to redefine these wants in order to breathe new life into them.

For example, why wouldn't you include love in the doctrines of your legal, economic, and social systems? Would it be so terrible to include love in your laws, currency, and customs, which would form the best expressions of yourselves? Indeed, not at all, for love is always involved in creating your future. So why not include it in your governmental edicts? Would you have only your tree huggers wanting love? Indeed, only your worst skeptics and unloved-feeling individuals would find reason to leave it out. Therefore, you'd do them a favor to bring it in!

Love incorporates moral authority

So what's wrong with including love in your Constitution? This may sound outlandish, but it wouldn't if you consider that love is something that would also do well to be redefined. The definition would require constancy of purpose in helping all creatures to thrive, and call on the better natures of human beings to do so.

We suggest *love* is best defined as *the moral authority that permits individuals a means to invoke the word, actions, and intent of their Personal God — their essence — in the service of self and others.*

Did you think we'd say "nurture and provide care for all individuals?" Indeed, we wouldn't. For your current expressions of love do not always follow the healthiest ways of spirit, and when you believe that you must love unconditionally, you are only half right. This definition does not include the ability to allow individuals to take responsibility for the repercussions of their actions.

In this, we will introduce a new word — *response-ability* — *the ability for individuals to enjoy the responses to the actions they choose.* In this, individuals need the ability to respond to their life situations in healthy or unhealthy ways. When you deny the ability to choose responses to their lives, you cripple them. We will explain.

Take, for example, a mother who is in a welfare system where she is only provided income for as many children as she has, instead of the means to help her know her true potential. She may not be fulfilling her potential, and may want to have a better life, but the only way she may know how to do so is to have more children, since that is what your current social programs often promote. We suggest that you love her enough to want the best things for her. In this, you'll want to find ways to assist in her way of spirit, the way she would find if she weren't encumbered by a system that tells her the only way she can support herself is to have children.

Do you understand what a disservice that is? We're not at all saying that welfare is ill-placed in every situation, just in those that deprive individuals of choices in which they may find and follow their desires and develop their extraordinary gifts.

In this, you need to make sure she has options, those you lovingly provide that nurture her way of spirit. Why would you do anything less? Because you've adopted a definition of love that is ill-defined and ill-suited for your society.

Response-ability leads to fulfillment

Love is sometimes tough because it wants to help make you, and others, response-able. The mother we just described has her way of spirit to follow and responds to her call of spirit in various ways. We suggest that you provide her new ways to follow her way of spirit. This would include educational choices, ways to make money while in school, and ways to find her passions: to instill response-ability in her life so she can fulfill her destiny, in a sense. In this way, she learns what her deeper purpose in life is. We're not at all saying there's no value in her current way of life—there is *great* value—only that the potential for facilitating choices that enable personal fulfillment is so sadly overlooked that it would be a crime to continue in this way.

We suggest, therefore, you adopt a new definition to include the words "and justice for all," for that will be exactly what you get when you include response-ability in your definition of love. For when you love someone, you want them to enjoy *your* way of spirit and *theirs*, correct? No. You want them to connect with *their* way of spirit to the extent that it matters not what *your* way of spirit is. So let go of individuals who you love to extinction, and learn to love them in ways that provoke their deepest fulfillment.

Love yourself first

We will give another example. Say you've come across a wonderful new way of looking at the world and you want others to feel the same passion you feel about it. What do you do? Do you implore them to listen? Do you impassively sit by and watch them ignore you? Your way of spirit will tell you exactly what to do. Do you want others to know about your ideas or not? Maybe you do and maybe you don't. The train of thought is interesting, but do you really need to share it?

We suggest you may not. What are you really looking for? Indeed, you're looking for validation from others, perhaps even love from others. However, you don't need their validation or love, only the love for yourself that fully accepts who you are.

As you begin to follow your way of spirit, you'll
find a love for yourself that is in many ways
independent of the love you seek from others.

We will make a comparison that may sound silly at first, but you'll understand it when we finish. Let's compare a boy of sixteen and a boy of twelve. The twelve year-old wants a new bike. That's fine, twelve year-olds like bikes, but some sixteen year-olds are too cool for bikes. So why would a sixteen year-old—with the way society beckons him to have a car so he can make out with his girlfriend—want with a bike?

He may want a bike to get around town, or he may have a desire to fix the bike and find out how it works. He may not know it yet, but he may become a great engineer in the future, and the bike would provide important training. Why would he therefore listen to individuals who tease him about the bike? If he truly loves himself, he wouldn't care what anyone says about his bike. Indeed, self-love is an important part of the way of spirit.

Again, we want to remind you that the way of spirit is yours and yours alone, so trust it to beckon to you in every way so as to find your best expressions and find yourself in love with yourself. For, indeed, you want to hear that, and you must. For what good is it if you love others but don't love yourself? That's why you've had so many problems with loving others: you need to love yourself first.

When you fall in love with your authentic self, you *always* include your Personal God, your essence, for this is the source of your natural intent, which informs your natural desires and wants. So do so.

Breathe in essence

We suggest you begin by allowing yourself a healthy dose of acceptance of your best self—your essence self—which is always closer than your heartbeat, for it is the source that makes them possible. What better way to do so than to acknowledge essence in every breath?

We call this *sontering—breathing in essence*.[5] Sontering has many benefits, including the ability to connect with the *fealing tone—a means to identify and interpret energy*—of your essence, as well as almost anything, although this will take practice. In

---

[5] See the Sonter (Breathe in Essence) practice on page 191.

doing so, it will remind you that everything in and around you is, indeed, essence.

Sontering, indeed, goes both ways, as essence sonters you in ways that you'll find most beautiful, as we have a breath of you in every moment. So while you sonter us, know we sonter you as well, as we love you, and we want to fill ourselves with you. So do so, and sonter each other, your world, your beautiful creations in spirit, in physical reality, in your days, nights, and your wonderful expressions of love. You always, indeed, want us in your lives, so let us in.

We essences always want you in our lives as well, even though you may not realize it, and will always assist. We want to provide you the best breath of livelihood you can possibly imagine. So trust that you will learn to incorporate your best selves, and your essence will always assist.

Make your livelihood a fulfilling one

Sontering is a way to find your best, most authentic self in every moment, and this also applies to your job. It provides you a means to breathe in ways to make your livelihood a wonderfully fulfilling one. And why wouldn't you have this? If you don't enjoy your work, you need to find ways to do so. We will assist, for your work, as we've said, is the most important thing you can do to allow a fulfilling life. Therefore, if you're not doing what you're passionate—*truly* passionate—about, you are not following your way of spirit.

Try to relax your expectations about why you're doing what you're doing in terms of your current job. We understand you need to pay your bills. But you can trust that when you wake up to your best self, you will find ways to pay your bills in more fulfilling ways. For why wouldn't you be allowed this? Because you've been trained from birth to toe the line and become robots willing to work on any assembly line that big brother assigns you. We're not exaggerating.

You have been raised to believe that your needs come second, but you're mistaken, your needs come first. And doing what you love is key to getting your needs met.

Again, the way to get out from under a job that you despise is to learn to follow your way of spirit, for when you do, things work out. That's correct, they just work out. You will also find that your contrary self, indeed, will help make you aware of new options and new choices that you couldn't see before.

You must learn to trust your inner contrary voice as the best authority in your way of spirit. It will say things like: "Do you have your resume up to date? Because you're going to need it!" And it will say, "Don't take that job, you'll hate it, even though you think you won't." And your contrary self will say, "Do you really expect that that uniform will suit you? You look terrible in it." Therefore, sontering your contrary self is a great way to find a new, more fulfilling job. So then, how do you find your new job? Here's how.

Appreciate your gifts

First, appreciate your many gifts. The gifts you have are the ones you've had your entire life. Take into consideration the gifts that you were born with—compassion, trust, playfulness—and those you've learned, such as proper etiquette and respect for others. You can bring these gifts into any work situation, for these are the core elements of any work situation: what you bring to bear in your world are the foundations of what makes human beings great.

So trust in these core values, and trust that they will assist you always, for the way of spirit insists on some things that you'll find wonderfully traditional in spite of what you might think. The way of spirit builds on what you know, not what you don't know. You'll do well to build on what you know about the world, to seek its proper ways, and to respect it, and it, in turn, will respect you and allow your best way of spirit.

Now, once you understand that you have much to offer in a new job, you must then build upon the skills you have in order to become the proper individual for the job. This can occur on your job, for while you may think that you need to be perfectly suited for any job, you don't. Your employer would much rather hire a wonderful, well-adjusted person to train than a surly person who has more applicable skills or experience.

For why wouldn't you create a job that you love, and a boss that you admire to assure you get the best training and the best job? Indeed, a willingness to learn is an admirable thing, more so than being a know-it-all. So, in a sense, the employer is you, and they will help your entry into your way of spirit. Indeed, that's their job, so trust that they will.

We also suggest that you offer to work extra hours. This may seem unfair, but why wouldn't you want to if you do what you truly love? Why wouldn't you want to do more than your "fair share"? That's right: because you have a *desire* to do it. This is the point.

The way of spirit calls to you to do what you love, and
do it with dignity, purpose, fulfillment, and fun.
The way of spirit is FUN!

So if you don't want to work extra hours on a job that you love, you're not following your way of spirit. We're not suggesting that you exhaust yourself—there is a balance—but trust that you'll want to exact whatever amount is fair from your paycheck and leave the rest to fulfilling your intent, for that's exactly what you'll be doing: you will fulfill the reasons why you chose to become physical.

We suggest that you'll provide a great example for others to follow as well, for you'll find a way to tell them about your insights, and assist individuals in their way of spirit. Be an example in your world. Your world sorely needs them. For when you follow your way of spirit, you assist everyone. You can simply tell them to find a job that they love. There is perhaps nothing more that you could say. But above all, trust that an important part of your way of spirit is to assist others with theirs, and the way you can do that is to be happy following yours.

Some things will be easy, some will take effort

We also suggest that your way of spirit is a most convenient one. The things you do should come easily, though you need to find truly fulfilling tasks and education with regard to your work. The way you have been raised is to take the easy path, and you might call this effortlessness, but you'd be incorrect. The way of spirit includes work, and that is sometimes difficult, for at times you need to challenge yourself. So why not do so?

Why wouldn't you want to challenge yourself to be a better, happier individual? Indeed the effort and education you choose will help you enjoy the work you love. So don't shy away from work, or effort, or further education. Indeed, your education will continue long after you're dead, so you may as well get used to it now! We trust you will.

Now, with all that said, we want very much to assure you that you're doing fine exactly the way you are now. Life is contradictory in that respect—you're always both perfect and imperfect, changing and standing still—and the way of spirit is no different. So don't feel you *have to* improve yourself— you don't—but do feel you *can* improve yourself in order to get happier, that's all.

You can count on your essences to assist, for we enjoy the challenge. We love to sit and file our nails on Cloud Nine, but that gets so very dull sometimes. So send us something to do, and we will love you for it. Of course, we always love you, so do what you will, and trust that we'll help you also by simply letting you beautifully create however you wish, as long as you're happy.

The keys to your happiness are in your way of spirit, and in this you only need to trust that you are loved as well as blessed.

Key Ideas: The Way of Spirit Will Find You

- Your desires are natural impulses in tune with your essence, and the healthiest expressions of your selfhood.
- *Passion* is what gets you excited in the spiritual sense and nudges you towards your desires.
- *Love* is best defined as the moral authority that permits you to invoke the innate intent of your Personal God in order to change your world.
- *Response-ability* is the ability for individuals to enjoy the responses to the actions they choose. When you deny this ability, you cripple them.
- Sontering is a way to find your best, most authentic self

in every moment. (See the Sonter—Breathe in Essence practice on page 191.)

- You've been raised to believe that your needs come second, but your needs come first. Doing what you love is key to getting your needs met.
- If you don't love your current job, make an effort to find one you do. Your natural gifts—like compassion, trust, playfulness, etiquette, and respect for others—are the foundation for any new work situation.
- When you follow your way of spirit, things work out.
- An important part of your way of spirit is to assist others with theirs. The way to do so is to be happy following yours.

Chapter 6: Trust in Your Innate Goodness

T he way the spirit world works is the way *you* work. Your essence guides you, but in ways that are so accommodating that you might think you're the one doing the guiding. And what else would you expect from essence, who only wishes to serve?

Indeed, you wouldn't want it to tell you what to do all the time: you need to call the shots, too. Your ego self has the gift of free will, which allows you to make your own choices in life. However, your essence self makes constant suggestions through your impulses, dreams, and intuitions—it really does nothing more than that—and you'll do well to listen, so as to follow your way of spirit, the best path for you. So do so.

Essence supports you in amazing ways

The spirit world works in "strange and mysterious ways." You've heard this used to describe God, and that's exactly why we use this expression: because your essence constantly works to support you, often in amazing ways. We will say more about this later, but for now, it's important to realize that there's also a version of God who is the Totality of All Things, All Probabilities, All That Is. So you may think of yourself in relation to God on three "levels" of being that exist at same time:

- The everyday God-in-training—the you who makes choices based on your way of spirit (your ego self)
- The mediating Personal God—the "spiritual suggestion box" who helps guide you (your essence self)
- All That Is

These distinctions are important, because when we discuss God, we sometimes need to be clear about which level we are referring to.

Every action has probabilities built in

Now, it is also important to understand that within All That Is, there is an infinite array of choices you and your essence can make. What this means is that you exist within a vast set of *probability fields* in which your every choice has an effect on the outcome of every event in your life and those around you.

> *Probabilities are the way*
> *things are likely to go.*

You can imagine that within All That Is, sometimes you think they're going one way, but they go another, and another, and another, until Infinity. And inherent in any situation—in every ghastly or wonderful experience—are built-in probabilities that things will go differently. And when you understand this, you will have the ability to really get the ideas we're about to tell you, for they're very important.

*Every action has probabilities built in, and every
situation can go in any direction at any time, no
matter how improbable it may be.*

For example, say you're walking down the street and see
a parked car with its headlights on. In one probability, you
don't even notice it, and think nothing of it.

In another probability, you *do* notice that the car has its
lights on, and you have the ability to turn the lights off. This
would benefit the individual whose car is in danger of finding
its battery dead. In both scenarios, you have the ability to help
the individual, whether it is by leaving the car alone and
safely parked, or, in a small act of kindness, by reaching in and
turning off the headlights.

Your actions matter

In either scenario, you have the ability to move the world
in ways that are beneficial. This is the natural order of things:
to benefit. So when you perform random acts of kindness, or
planned actions of benevolence, you perform in ways that are
aligned with the world.

In this case, you benefit the planet by allowing the car to
conserve energy, and you benefit the individual when you
prevent him from having a dead battery. *You* also benefit,
perhaps more than anyone else in the situation, because you
are following your way of spirit.

And you can think of acts of kindness as helpful to your
Personal God, too, for it looks kindly upon them. Indeed,
that's what we're here for. Your Personal God nudges you to
move in these directions constantly. So the suggestions of
essence will always—*always*—beautifully portray innate
goodness through the loving spirits we are, and *you* are.

Therefore, your energies mingle with your mediating essence energies to create a wonderful collaboration in spirit. You can also imagine that All That Is, indeed, is informed of this, for all things are interconnected. So when you engage in works of charity or other forms of spiritual activity, you love the world and all things. You are intimately interested in doing so because you *are* all things.

As we have said, you are Gods-in-training. This can be somewhat confusing, so we'd like to sort things out for you, for misunderstanding this idea can result in a great deal of disharmony.

When we say, "You are Gods-in-training," we mean that on your level of Godhood, you are learning to be your essence-level God. In some respects they are the same, but in other respects they're not. For your essence-level Godhood can be considered your future self, in some respects, although you coexist in time. Essence is not interested in time and space like you are, because essence exists primarily in areas of consciousness that are outside of your space-time construction. So you're correct if you've guessed the next part.

Your experience of time and space is part of what
you are learning to manipulate in terms of
physical reality as Gods-in-training.

Now, let's return to the probabilities already in progress in your car scenario.

Let's say the car is parked on a street in which the dog catcher lives. When you reach into the car to turn the lights off, you get a scare, as you didn't notice there's a dog in the car, who growls at you. The dog has no tags and is not licensed. You suspect that the dog may be dangerous, but you don't know for sure. The dog also looks very sweet, but you would do well to not try to find out. You also notice that the dog has not taken his medicine. We know you can't know this for sure, but we're saying that you'll know instinctively that the dog hasn't been cared for.

The dog is not licensed, is potentially dangerous, and is not being cared for. What do you do? Do you go to the dog catcher's house and tell him or her about the dog?

Indeed, you would. For your wanting to save the trouble of doing what you know inside is the right thing is laziness, and not wanting to assist because you think that the dog or the owner would not like it would be an even worse offense. You would have the ability to help the dog, help the potential children in the dog's path, and help the owner by allowing him or her to get the dog the proper care it needs, for the owner needs help, too. They may not know what is required and want to help the dog, but need guidance. And that is why—as you explore the probable outcomes—you would want to report the dog to the dog catcher and save him the trouble of having to find the dog in a more protracted way. For your way of spirit sometimes needs to allow for guidance, as well as *policy* and *policing*.

Show respect through policy and policing

Policy and policing are similar in the respect that policy sets the rules and policing encourages some to follow them. We say *some* people, meaning that they won't always want to be policed, as this would intrude on what they consider to be their fun, but in some respects, this is incorrect. The fun sometimes comes from being policed, and when you avoid policing, you ruin their fun as well as their response-ability.

For why would anyone truly want to beat up old ladies and snatch their purses? Do you really believe this is fun for them, not to mention for the old ladies? Indeed, this is so very *not* fun that you'd do everyone a valuable service by allowing yourself to be more police-like at times and spare us the stories about wanting to allow individuals their rights to express themselves. For your ways of spirit don't promote one individual's fun at the expense of another, and we'll tell you why.

When individuals don't get the respect they need, they turn on others. The respect they need is what you can give them, only you may not know how. When you don't correct an individual—whether they are two or twenty years old—they don't get the respect they need from you. Theories abound with regard to respect and what it is, but we will define respect as *fondness—not necessarily love—but fondness that promotes response-ability.*

When you respect someone, you become familiar with them in subtle and profound ways.

We will give you an example. Say that you have a food tray that you will give to a very old person, and you have the ability to put flowers on it. Why would you do this? To show respect and what you think would be a nice way to treat them.

Do you call this policing? Perhaps not, but why not? When you police things, you provide the flower on the tray, in a sense, for individuals who need the attention. This includes individuals who need to be shorn of their locks on their entry to prison, or someone who needs the benefit of your spoken word when they do wrong at the expense of other's well-being. For acting out to get attention has created so many merciless actions that some are considered brutal by even the worst offenders, not only by the law-abiding citizens who pay taxes for someone else to take them on.

Indeed, *you need to take on these kinds of individuals, and the way you do this is through your acts of respect, kindness, and mercy.* You each have the ability to intervene on lives in ways that are greatly—indeed, *divinely*—inspired, so do so. We will give you another example.

The Tale of the Quarreling Princesses

There is a cottage by a stream, and the cottage is run by three princesses. They are constantly quarreling with each other, so you, a prince, can't stand going to visit, but you allow yourself to do so because you want to marry one and get the princess' cottage.

Why would you do that? Because you don't respect the princesses: you only want their money. And why would you do *that*? Because you're not following your way of spirit.

Indeed, why would you not follow your way of spirit? Because you haven't connected with the idea that you're here to perform good works, and you have the response-ability to suggest to the princesses that you would not want to marry any of them given their terrible habit of quarreling.

So you'd do well to take the approach of caring enough to tell them they are limiting their options by constantly quarreling. Indeed, one of them may want to marry you, so you'd do well to get the facts straight. And you'd do what we would call *policing in love and without fear*. Since the abbreviation PILAWF would be terrible, we'll call it *policing in love*, and that's exactly what your way of spirit calls you to do.

Policing in love is what you're here to do, as well as to enjoy yourself. And who says that policing in love can't be fun, too? Indeed, why wouldn't your prince love to tell the princesses what the way of spirit calls him to?

Indeed, he could say, "Well, Your Royal Pains in the Butt! What do you want to quarrel about today? Should we carry the *venison* to the neighbors or should we carry the *chickens*? Indeed, why would you quarrel about something so ridiculous? Indeed, no one will want to marry you, given your silly arguments. Certainly not *me!*"

And what would be more fun than to see the looks on those three princesses' faces when that truly wonderful suggestion comes their way? Indeed, now *that* is *fun!*

We suggest that you've learned some very bad habits. We will try to set the record straight for once and for all, because you need this information desperately.

Acts of kindness have great power

The way you sometimes consider kindness is in the most wrong way you could possibly imagine. That you would let that poor dog suffer, that poor dog owner suffer, the poor princesses suffer, the poor woman in her wheelchair without a flower on her tray suffer because she doesn't think anyone loves her—these are some of the worst ways to not show kindness that you could possible imagine. And yet, you consider yourselves to be such kind people.

Do you see the folly in this? Why would you possibly want to endanger a child under the guise of wanting to allow people to do their own thing? Indeed, this is the most dangerous way to live that we would imagine, and we imagine a great deal. This leads us back to probabilities, and your way of spirit.

> *When you perform an act of kindness—indeed, an act of policing in love—you create a rich set of probabilities around yourself. The way you can think of this is as "the Force."*

Remember Luke Skywalker's way of handling himself? He was told to summon his courage and blast the evil Death Star out of the sky. Indeed, he followed his way of spirit, and "the Force was strong in him," in Obi-Wan Kenobi's terms.

Why was the Force so strong in him? Because he followed his intent, left his home, left his family, and faced the challenge of the dark forces of nature. This is exactly what you do every single day when you walk down the street or sit at your computer. You also do this when you allow your way of spirit to contend with what you may consider the dark forces of nature. And when you do, you connect with the greater energy of All That Is.

Do you know why? Did you notice that the word "evil" in the earlier paragraph is spelled like a regular old word? Indeed, that's because that's exactly what it is: a word.

The evil you know is a fashionable illusion designed to enable you to find your way of spirit. When you find *the way*, you know it. You know it with all your heart and soul, because All That Is is innately Good.

That's right. There is no evil with a capital E, as if there's some Dark Lord who prevails as much as Goodness. You can trust that when you follow your way of spirit, you will do only good. This is another reason why you chose to become physical: to remind you that as Gods-in-flesh, you are Goodness Personified. In this, you will be the best and most fulfilled individual you can be.

For when you don't take action, you're not happy because you ignore the call of your essence self in ways that are sad. That's what you are when you don't invest in your world, in your lives, and in yourself. For to become an island—and think that the world doesn't need you—does you and the world a terrible disservice.

For you are Goodness, you are Love, you are the Obi-Wans and Darth Vaders of your world, and you only need to choose. The way of spirit suggests in your every breath which way to go, as the path of light is the only way towards All That Is.

For there is no evil at that level—only at your physical god level—so you can take that to the bank, as well as perform acts of power.

You will find that aligning with All That Is is
fulfilling and wondrous, dear Gods-in-training.

You'd do well to remember this! *That*, after all, is what we're here for, us essences: to remind you of your innate Goodness in a very big way. What more could we do for you? Indeed just ask.

But be assured that wanting only fame and fortune is not the point. The way of spirit doesn't like that—it likes sloppiness, and bleeding, and all kinds of horrible things. So get used to this, and we'll suggest again that you've signed up for it, indeed!

Key Ideas: Trust in Your Innate Goodness

- You can think of yourself in relation to God on three "levels" of being that exist simultaneously:

  o The everyday God-in-training—the "you" who makes choices based on your way of spirit (your ego self)

  o The mediating Personal God who functions as a "spiritual suggestion box" who helps guide you (your essence self)

  o All That Is

- *Probabilities* are the way things are likely to go. Every action has probabilities built in and every situation can go in any direction at any time, no matter how improbable it may be.

- The natural order of things is to benefit. Your essence continually nudges you to choose beneficial outcomes. Choosing them creates a rich set of probabilities around you.

- *Policy* sets the rules and *policing* encourages some to follow them.

- *Policing in love* shows others respect in ways that are aligned with All That Is.

- *Respect* is the need to attract fondness in a way that promotes response-ability.

- You need to take on individuals acting in harmful ways. The way to do this is through your acts of respect, kindness, and mercy.

- All That Is is innately Good. To align with your innate Goodness as a God-in-training, and perform fulfilling acts of power and service, are why you chose to become physical.

Chapter 7: Trust in the Power of Probabilities

I n following your way of spirit, you will realize probabilities moving in deeply satisfying directions. "The water of eternal life" verse in your Bible accurately describes the infinite nature of probabilities, and the infinite nature of yourself.

The way you can think of probabilities is that everything that *can* happen, *will*. This doesn't mean that you'll scratch your head in one scenario and in another you won't: it doesn't work to this degree of detail. Mostly, the probabilities of whether or not you will take a certain job or live in another place creates main sets of probabilities that serve as potential paths for you to take.

These probabilities will make themselves known in your intuition, and your essence will suggest certain paths that would be the most fulfilling.

You have many paths available to you in every moment, and you have the choice to follow the paths that your essence suggests, or not.

These paths are not as linear as you'd think the paths would be: after all, they're paths, right? But they're not linear in probabilities, so we will explain.

Probabilities allow many paths at once

Probabilities allow for a great many varieties of paths. Some paths intersect in ways you'll find astonishing, as some of your movies portray perfectly. In some scenes, the characters will take one path, in some scenes they'll take another. This is exactly the way probabilities work in real life, for you have *probable selves* who experience certain probabilities that you don't, and they will experience certain paths sometimes, too. But in every case, they are *you*.

> *While you can think of them as*
> *probable selves, keep in mind that*
> *they are real in every way—*
> *as real as you!*

You have the ability to see through their eyes at any time, as you sometimes do, for instance, in your dreams. This is yet another way to understand that you are part of a larger multidimensional being—your essence self.

Now, you also look at your dreams in astonishing—as well as frightful—ways at times. Various scenarios may play out in your dreams in order to suggest what to do or not do based upon a probable future event, for example, avoiding a plane flight or not taking a new job. Trusting your dreams is so important that we will devote an entire chapter to it, but for now, we want to impress on you the multidimensional nature of your essence self and how probable realities play out in your inner world of your dreams and imaginations.

Your essence self is so vast that in addition to your probable selves, you have, as we've said, other life-"times," too, which we call focuses of attention who live in other time frameworks that exist alongside of your own.

Much like your Star Trek heroes on television, your essence is able to perceive different space-time constructions including those within other dimensions.

Your essence is so vast that you simultaneously exist in many different kinds of inner realms.

Your probable selves exist in a variety of times, spaces, and dimensions—more than you could possibly imagine and then some. So when you step into your dream space, you experience many different realities and probabilities that you would do well to remember sometimes. In this, your dreams provide very practical and healthy ways to explore who you are in your vastness.

Who *you* are in the vastness of Self

The way to determine who you are is, therefore, a big challenge. For who you are in your physical reality is only the tip of the iceberg. Indeed, why wouldn't an iceberg show everything that it has beneath its tip? Because it only needs to show what's on top. Indeed, there wouldn't be an iceberg if it were to expose all of itself above the water.

In similar ways, you expose only your physical self so as to experience the physical world you live in now. And this is the point: it's important to *not* allow too much interest in other probable selves and lifetimes so as to detract from this one. But it is important to realize the vastness of self so that you may interact with spirit in fulfilling ways. In this, probable selves can assist.

Take, for instance, a probable you who wasn't able to finish high school. Can you imagine the life this person has led? We're using the example to illustrate that you would not exist in exactly the way you do now. Not having a high school diploma or equivalent significantly discourages some probabilities from taking effect. This is the point: the choices you make in your life occur in ways that suit you, and to not have a diploma is somewhat the same as having one, but allows you to obtain some experiences that are different.

So you have a probable self who didn't get a high school diploma who is learning *for you*—and we mean that so strongly we will italicize it, *for you*—that you need to get a diploma in order to allow greater opportunities for making a good living. And that probable self informs *your* every day in every way, and tells you what you need to do. That probable self is informed by your physically focused self as well, as is every probable self in every scenario that you can dream of, which includes every lifetime and every dimension you have chosen to experience. Indeed, you are vast.

So who could argue with what you get, in terms of multidimensional information, in your way of spirit? For you have the best, most wonderfully challenging information that you could possibly imagine, that indeed comes from *you*.

And who loves you more than your essence self? Indeed, no one.

You deserve help from essence

We essences are you as well. We are the sum of millions of *yous* who provide the best sources of information possible. For we read you, we know you, we live you, we are you in every way you can possibly imagine, and then some.

> *So don't wonder if we're here to serve*
> *you, we are you. Why would you not*
> *want to serve yourself?*

Indeed, because you may not feel you deserve it. We believe that your training has been so very erroneous so as to completely cripple some individuals, and hopefully this doesn't apply to you.

If you want to be crippled, then you can continue to absorb the many messages that your culture tells you to believe: that you are flawed from birth, that you are flawed *before* birth, that you are flawed if you don't look a certain way, that you are flawed if you *do* look a certain way, and so on.

Your self-trust has been so diminished by this propaganda that you sometimes need a fix. The fix is to sonter—breathe in your essence self—which we introduced in a previous chapter and you can practice at any time.[6] We suggest that you do so regularly in order to appreciate the wonderment that is you, and while you do, trust that your essences are breathing you in, too.

We help you to create *all* of your reality. As we said, your ego doesn't always *want* the reality it creates.

> *Trust that when you breathe in essence,*
> *you breathe in your world as well, and*
> *allow yourself to create in your world*
> *the things that you desire.*

In this, probabilities play an important part, for when you make the smallest movement in your world, you influence many probabilities. You can imagine them as fractals or psychic patterns in which the fragments closest to you are larger and the ones further away are smaller and more complex. The ones that you consider closer are the *most*

---

[6] See the Sonter (Breathe in Essence) practice on page 191.

probable probabilities, and the ones that are further away and more complex are your *least probable* probabilities. Both are determined by your choices, thoughts, and actions. Every one of your probabilities is possible, only more or less probable. So while anything is *possible*, some things are *more probable* than others.

Essence can do *anything*

While essence tends to do things in typical ways, they can do anything, and you would do well to remind yourself of this. The weird, seemingly improbable probabilities further away in your conceptualization are the ones you need to pay attention to sometimes, for your essence will help to correct things when you get bogged down in probabilities that won't aid in your fulfillment. We will explain.

Nothing can *permanently* harm you, because you, in essence, will never die. The ideas are complicated, so for now we will say that many of your worst fears come from the belief that your physical death is a kind of annihilation. Your physical body does die, but your essence body—which is the source of your physical body and your energetic body in the spiritual sense—can never be destroyed.

In your terms, you create harm when you allow yourself to think of yourself as *only* a physical, non-essence being. There's not any harm *in essence*, in a sense, because you will *in those terms* never be harmed nor die. *This is not to say that there isn't harm you can inflict on yourself and others,* as this is the journey you have chosen to take, but in essence, there is no physical harm. Getting to where you need to be in your beliefs is why you create harm, both physical and emotional. You experience harm to self and others because you have chosen to forget what you know as essence, and when you realize that, you want to end it.

Let go of your fear

Harming others and yourself is therefore a tricky subject, but we will offer this: letting go of your fear is the best thing you can do with this information.[7] Again, while there's no harm in the essence sense, there *is* harm in the physical sense. When you promote harm and suffering in yourself and others, you wallow in the fear that you're not spiritual, when indeed you are.

There are many ways that you can allow spiritual energy to assist in any suffering that you have created, including spontaneous healing of an illness. The way of spirit includes illness so that you will find ways to overcome it that aid in your growth. Illnesses *are* real, but they are also not harmful in larger terms because in the essence sense, there is no dying, just metamorphosis. In your Gods-in-training realm, there is physical death of the body. So we are talking on many levels here, and when we say there's no harm, we mean *in the essence world*.

> *So remember this: physical, emotional, and psychological harm can always be avoided, but you may not choose to do so for your own experiences as Gods-in-training.*

Spontaneous healing is one example in which you can avoid harm by allowing seemingly improbable events to

---

[7] See the Address and Release Your Fears practice on page 194.

occur. Spontaneous healing can occur when you open yourself up to the ways of health that your essence provides. As such, you only need to request essence's help, then allow. When you do, and when conditions are right, you are spontaneously healed. This is not to say this is always what you desire, as sometimes you want the illness so that you may learn from it.

There is never any reason to believe that in creating illness or suffering that you are somehow flawed or not spiritual: there is always purpose for it. But when this is not beneficial, or when the learning has taken place, essence will be there to assist. It will do so by inserting probabilities into your reality that fix the problem so rapidly you may not take notice. Sometimes you may create an illness, like a tumor, that will be repaired before you even realize it's there. In some cases, you will be healed, but you will hold onto the energy that surrounds the area so tightly that you will continue to experience the symptoms until you address the beliefs that are creating them.[8]

So probabilities are constantly changing, whether or not you notice. Essence takes note of everything you do in order to assist you in your probabilities, for it wants the best probabilities for you, indeed.

Surf the waves of your probable selves

Now, one way to think of yourself, then, is surfing the waves of the most fulfilling probable selves. This is the best metaphor in many ways, for surfing is an exhilarating thing, so you may consider yourself the Silver Surfer of the Cosmos.

---

[8] See the Identify, Define, and Effortlessly Address your beliefs (IDEA) practice on page 193.

You want to realize the best probabilities in order to get the most fulfilling experiences that your way of spirit will allow. So trust that your current life is chosen by you as essence in every single moment from a vast array of probable selves in this and other dimensions and timeframes.

And in this, you can rest assured that you are the most beloved, most wonderfully suited individual for your individual scene, and the scene is exactly suited for you as well. So when you trust essence in order to accomplish what you need to, you must therefore assume that you are truly remarkable. And indeed you are.

So trust that you'll do well in your world, for it will be exactly suited to your tastes and needs, whether or not you appreciate it.

Now, keep in mind that your probabilities constantly change around you depending on what you choose, and sometimes you are faced with choices that may harm others as well as yourself. The way we defined *harm* earlier was subtle, and it's important that you understand this, so we will make it a bit clearer for you so that you will make choices that will benefit yourself and others.

Your inner moral cooperative sense

When you harm another, you *violate* them, and that is recorded in consciousness. Everything is recorded in consciousness, because everything *is* consciousness. So when you do something that violates another, you allow what we would call an *imprint*, and that is an important thing to know.

Karma, in the way it's often considered, is a linear process where intent and actions of an individual influence their subsequent lifetimes in the form of rewards as well as punishment. But this belief doesn't allow for the idea that the violation can allow you to grow spiritually: you wouldn't need to in order to experience the rewards or punishments that result from your actions in consecutive lifetimes.

In other words, why wouldn't you want to learn from your violation so you, in any moment, don't do it again, therefore not cause harm, and grow in spirit? Indeed, you would want to find out what it was like on the receiving end, and avoid it if possible, would you not? After all, you are the world, and you would feel the pain of another were you to hurt them, indeed.

Because you as essence simultaneously exist in many probabilities, times, spaces, and dimensions, you have the ability to be aware of the violation—and the *potential* for violation—so as to make beneficial, non-violating decisions in your now. This can be considered your *inner moral cooperative sense*, because by choosing to not violate, you live in greater cooperation with All That Is.

So you can redefine *karma* as *an action propelled by the imprint of a violation to compel you to learn from your mistake. Therefore, when you violate another, you also violate yourself.* But you choose this, because you want to more fully realize the beautiful God that you are in the process of becoming. For, indeed, this is your way of spirit.

The Godliness you have inside *always* wants to express itself in ways you find wonderful. You can expect to have the help of your best probable selves in order to do this. So when we say that in doing good works you allow greater things to happen, we mean it in every way. For you'll find that when you follow your way of spirit, things go your way. In this, the sorrow and joy of the world will always be part of your physical reality, for very important reasons.

Key Ideas: Trust in the Power of Probabilities

- You have a vast number and variety of *probable selves* who simultaneously exist in many inner realms to explore "roads not taken" by you.

- Probable selves communicate with you in dreams and other altered states to provide you information regarding choices you may or may not want to make.

- Your essence self is so vast that in addition to your probable selves, you have other life-"times" —*focuses of attention*—who live in other time frameworks that exist alongside of your own.

- Essence can correct anything that is not aiding in your fulfillment by inserting seemingly improbable probabilities

- Harm and death occur in the physical realm, but not in the essence realm. You experience harm to remember that you are essence. It will help to let go of your fears about harm and death. (See the Address and Release Your Fears practice on page 194.)

- Essence can spontaneously heal and alleviate suffering by inserting probabilities that you may not notice.

- Because you as essence simultaneously exists in many probabilities, you have the ability to be aware of violation—and the potential for violation—to make beneficial, non-violating decisions in your now. This is your *inner moral cooperative sense.*

- *Karma* is an action propelled by the imprint of a violation to compel you to learn from your mistake, because when you violate another, you also violate yourself.

Chapter 8: Sorrow and Joy

"Picture yourself in a boat on a river with tangerine trees and marmalade skies." Indeed, your Beatles had it right when they recorded that song, for your boat on a river is your essence who carries you along.

Your essence will *always* get you to where you need to go, and will do so while it helps you create your reality in every way. The trees are your trees, the skies are your skies, and the way you sail through your world is as enchanting as you'll ever imagine. For everything in your world is a miracle created by essence exactly for you. The pain and the sorrows, too, are fulfilling parts of it.

That's right: pain and suffering are a natural part of your world, as difficult as they may be to understand at times. But they also make your bliss and joy possible. When you embrace this fact, you will have the foundation to follow your way of spirit and navigate your probable rivers in the most fluid ways possible. In this way, your suffering is also part of your joy.

When you realize this, you will have the best time on your boat of self, for to relieve suffering is the greatest joy on earth.

Sorrow is what you get when the world is in pain. No matter who is in pain, everyone suffers, because *the world is you*. We want to say this so very clearly that you'll not question the idea again, as you need to understand this.

The suffering of the world is yours

The world is you. Indeed, we suggest you watch your news with this mind so as to better understand the way your essence works. Why wouldn't everything you see be you? Why wouldn't everything in your mind be you? Why wouldn't everything in the world be you in some way? Indeed, you have more reasons to believe the world is you than you have to believe it isn't.

Let's explore an example. Say you want to visit Paris. The world exists in your home and outside it. The world is the way you get there. The world is what you see along the way. The world is the hotel you stay in. The world is the people you speak to. The world is the sights you see.

What would happen if you apply these principles to your everyday experiences? What would happen if you treat the images on your news the same way as your Paris trip? Because oftentimes they're sorrowful images, and you don't like that. You want the joy of Paris, but you don't want the sorrows on your television.

We so want to help end your suffering, but you don't always allow this. You also often fail to remember that you're the ones who help to create suffering in the first place. Why? So you could *remember* your divine self.

You create suffering because you have a great need to identify with essence in ways that you don't yet, but will once you get used to the idea.

Your monks and sages have it completely right: the suffering of the world is yours and you must embrace it in order to be fully human. Indeed, the way you go about this is to suffer *with* the sufferers and feel what they feel. In other words, you must learn to use your empathic sense to identify with them, to *feal—feel in real ways*—compassion, to "walk a mile in their shoes."

Why would you want to do this? Because *they are you!*

Your desires are in your joy and compassion

The world isn't a place based upon fairy tales. The world is different than any other space-time place in the Universe, as it is a special place where people as divine beings go to learn compassion. The way you do this is through your inner, intuitive senses, not your outer, physical senses.

If you believe that you suffer with others because you're afraid you'll be in their shoes someday, you would be mistaken, because you are *already* suffering in their shoes— you just don't realize it.

> *When you realize this very important point—*
> *that because you are them, you are already*
> *suffering—you will understand the world in*
> *terms you never did before.*

You will see it as a grand illusion, in some respects, and you will understand that you suffer with the intensity they do in ways that transcend your own beliefs about who you are and what you find important.

Indeed, you could use a dose of this important medicine, because it will enable you to see that the world does want to make you happy. You want the world to make you happy in certain ways, but the world can only do so in its own ways—ways that you deeply desire. To allow the world to do so, to bring you the most joy, you need to practice another important part of the way of spirit—*finding compassion*. We will explain.

Compassion is powerful

You need to find compassion in ways that you don't yet. First, realize that suffering will always continue in your world to some degree, for it comes with the territory, so to speak. Therefore, you can't always stop it, but since compassion will always be in your world as well, you can learn to use it.

Next, realize that compassion is what makes you the Divine beings that you are. Compassion is a Truth with a capital "T." As we've said, in many respects there are no truths, only beliefs. A Truth, in our terms, is something that transcends all probable realities in every dimension and every area of consciousness. In other words, it is an absolute.

Love—in our terms, not yours, as love is different in other areas of consciousness—is another Truth. Consciousness is another Truth. Tone is another. Potentiality is another, and so on. This is a big topic, so for now, imagine Compassion as something that transcends all probable realities in every dimension and every area of consciousness. And why wouldn't it? Indeed, we've told you that All That Is is innately Good, so why wouldn't Compassion be an essential part of your Universe? Indeed, it exists in all things, and that includes *you*.

Many of you truly want to help people, but you've been taught that this is folly because you're all doomed to suffer—through punishment for your sins or natural catastrophe—based on the religious and scientific views of your supposedly

flawed natures. And you provide yourselves constant
evidence of this all around you. Still, why wouldn't you want
to help even if you were doomed? For your expressions of
helpfulness and compassion are sorely needed by you and the
world, too.

Compassion heals you and the world

When you block compassion, you block your way of
finding happiness, and then your way of spirit is only half
alive, in some respects. For when you live in ways that are
truly compassionate, you truly live. That is the point.

> *Trust your compassionate self to*
> *invoke your Personal God, and your*
> *way of spirit will fully blossom.*

You don't need to go to a third-world country or spend
time in a leper colony. You only need to trust that the world
will provide you with opportunities to engage in simple acts
of courage and compassion where you find them. In this, you
assist the entire world.

The way you can open to your compassion is a remarkable
thing. For instance, what do you get when you take your ego
self out of the picture? You get essence. You get divinity. You
get the hell out of your own way. For what is hell, really? It's
only a projection of your own ego self, the self that is needy,
the self that wants things it can't always have, the self that is
so ego-bound that it seeks joy in ways that actually makes it
unhappy.

On the other hand, when you express your compassion in
the world, your joy will follow, and you will find that your
ways truly become expressions of the divine. As a result, you

create heaven on earth—a joy that ripples out to affect the world, too. For you are the world, are you not?

So the way you can think about your compassionate self is as your best self, your essence self. When you follow the way of spirit and remove the artifacts of beliefs about what you want the world to give you, you remove fear and doubt in ways you will find funny, too. You will remove things in ways that will make you giddy with pleasure—your funny habits, anxieties, and finding fault with others and with yourself. These are all things you'd like to remove, wouldn't you?

Indeed, the way of spirit allows this to occur in ways that are most healthy. When you remove your fears and defenses, you'll also create more health in your body than you could ever imagine. For your body, mind, emotions, and essence are all invested in your experiences, and together, seek to provide ways to reap more rewards in your body and mind than you could ever expect by taking a drug or mending a scar. The way of spirit will rehabilitate you in every way, for it naturally promotes joy, health, and fulfillment.

*Finding joy is the result of following your
way of spirit. If you are not joyful, then
you're not doing it right.*

When you do it right, you will reap the rewards that you'll truly desire and send your fears packing. Fear is only your "wanting ways" that lead to chronic unhappiness. So stop wanting the things that never truly fulfill you, and start wanting what you *desire*. This includes compassion.

Find compassion for yourself first

We suggest you find compassion first for yourself. Indeed, the way many of you have been raised is—as we've said—flawed, and you'll do well to throw out most everything and start again. Begin with the idea that you were born in a state of Love and Compassion that you will never leave, for that is what essence knows and you have forgotten.

We will invoke a wonderful old expression: to know you is to love you, and to know yourself is to love yourself. We will also repeat the words of your Jesus, "Love your neighbor as you love yourself." For not loving yourself gets in the way of loving your neighbors. So you need to start with yourself. Here's how.

Throw out everything you've learned about the nature of sin.

Sin isn't the thing you do to make others unhappy.
Sin is what you do to make yourself unhappy. Your
beliefs about sin are flawed, not you.

The "flaws" you have are the things that you have not addressed—the fears, the lack of compassion, the anxieties—and they are all necessary for you to learn to find compassion for yourself. They serve to get your attention in order to address your fears.[9] That's all they are.

So when you feel fearful or anxious, or want to project your own inadequacies on someone, you must first take stock and *feal* the excitement of your inner being and trust that you're only looking for us—your divine essence selves—to incorporate into your lives. For we are always here, always

---

[9] See the Address and Release Your Fears practice on page 194.

love you, and always want to assist in the creation of the things you desire.

So love yourself and know we want only the very best things for you, in spite of how you sometimes feel about yourself. In this, you can count on the fact that you are always—*always*—loved.

So take it from us: you only need to set aside your perceived flaws, feal the love and compassion we have for you, and embrace it for yourself and others. When you do, you will overcome self-imposed limitations and private hells you create when you only distrust and fear.

Here's a time-tested way to help rid you of your fears, and promote a deep sense of joy: meditate.

When you meditate, you trust your essence to take over and remind you of your Divinity.

Meditation doesn't require that you sit on a mountaintop, or in a cross-legged position. Meditation is to simply relax into yourself, close your eyes, breathe in your essence (sonter), and experience the fealing tone of your Being, your Personal God.[10] That's all. The way you can imagine essence is as a tender touch, a compress on your forehead that calms and soothes you, a light fine wine to resolve your tensions, remove your fears, and indeed, that's exactly what your essence is.

Why do you think the Buddha smiles when he meditates? Because he enjoys the state of *resting in essence*. So trust that you, too, can find the joy of the Buddha as easily when you close your eyes and rest in your divine being. In this way, you'll find your compassionate self, promote your own well-being, and create joy in the world. We trust you will.

_____

[10] See the Rest in Rose practice on page 192.

Key Ideas: Sorrow and Joy

- You are the world, and the world is you, even the pain and suffering.

- To embrace sorrows with compassion is to be fully human, to identify with your essence self, and make your joy possible.

- Compassion transcends all probable realities in every dimension in every area of consciousness. It is an absolute, a Truth with a capital "T".

- When you express your compassion in the world, your joy—a desire—will follow.

- Your "flaws" are only things that you have not addressed—the fears, the lack of compassion, the anxieties—that get your attention so that you may address and release your fears.

- When you feel fearful or anxious, take stock and *feal*—feel in real ways—the love and compassion essence always has for you and others.

- Meditation—to sit in stillness and rest in the fealing tone of your Personal God—will help you find compassion and promote a deep sense of joy. (See the Rest in Rose practice on page 192.)

Chapter 9: Find Your Personal God

"The way of seeking" would do well to be called "the way of finding," for constant seeking is a problem that many people have. We walk among you, us gods, and you would do well to pay attention, for you have not yet learned to follow the way of spirit. Instead, you have sought, as well as found, some things that aren't working for you very well.

One important way we essences communicate things is through your contrary selves, as we've said, but you don't always pay attention. Instead, you pay attention to what your ego self believes we want you to have.

In this, you've been corrupted, and we don't use this word too strongly, for your corruption runs very deep. For you would do well to learn that you are *much* more than your ego, and that you have access to your own Personal God.

Your unnecessary wants do not suit you

We are not very interested in what you want to buy, or what you want to wear. We're only interested in *you*. So why do you want to insist on things that serve as serious distractions from your works in the world? Indeed, you don't desire many things, but you've been taught that you do. You would do well to *geaniusly—combining your innate spiritual wisdom and genetic codes inherent in your bodies*—provide yourself with better information than you do now. The word "genius" sometimes sounds like it comes from a source outside of you, but the genes in your body are essence, too, and provide introspective information that can be considered inspired.

You can choose to create a most superficial life in ways that you would find fulfilling in some respects, but on a deeper level, those choices don't always suit you. Indeed, the way of spirit suits you better, and again, you need to relearn what you've been taught.

In spite of your training, you've done a wonderful job thus far. Most of you have been taught the benefits of compassion. In this, the expression "Love your brother" is one of the best things you could include in your way of spirit. So trust that this is correct.

Also correct is, "Love in spite of hate." When you become overly separated from spirit, you will want things you don't desire, and in wanting those things, you will sometimes hate. And indeed, you're correct in your assumption that the wanting is what creates the hating, because you see the blocks to obtaining your wants as deserving of your antipathy rather than the gentle nudging of spirit towards your true desires. So when you learn to reconnect with spirit, you will no longer hate.

> *In spite of your desire for goodness in the world, it is the aftereffects of superficial wanting that lead to hatred, greed, and needless self-promotion.*

Wanting things that don't serve you, therefore, expresses itself in hatred and unhappiness. Wanting also extends into other physical realms in the many dimensions that you, as essence, live in, for karma happens in ways we've defined previously. So wanting affects many things, including other lifetimes.

While you may think that wanting things inappropriate for you is a small thing, it's not, and you can trust that you affect many millions of individuals when you do. This is important to note, because you need to think about the effects of your every action and learn that when you take action towards getting what you want, many others are affected in some way.

You are not an island in any sense of the word. In fact, as a God-in-training, you're well on your way to better understanding your Divine nature by reading this book. So don't despair: you want to change and that is a wonderful thing! So trust that when *we* want you to change, it's for a very good reason: because *you* wish to do so. We wouldn't waste our divine breath on just anyone! So keep reading, dear ones—we want to explore this good news further.

The Universe helps you to obtain your desires

Isn't it wonderful to know that your actions affect a vast majority of individuals in some way, however small? You'll do well to change your habits so you can do what you truly *desire* in your world, and not through the wants in the way you've become accustomed. Indeed, you've taught yourselves those things, no one else.

When we say, "You are the world," we don't want you to confuse this with narcissism, which incorporates the belief that your ego self is the most important, most central person in the world. There are many individuals who'd like to think that they are the center of your Universe, and indeed they'd be half right. Their ego self is the center of *their* Universe only, as is yours, but not the center of *the* Universe. So let's explore the differences.

The way you can think of yourself as the center of the Universe is as a plant that gets some light from the sun. The sun exists only for the plant, correct? No. The plant gets light from the sun that shines for *all*. The plant is one of many individuals who feed off the beautiful rays in order to live.

The same is inherent in your Universe. You are nurtured by the power of the Universe so that you can create a happy life. The plant is, too, and it shares the light with others, as you share the powers of the Universe with others in ways that don't intrude upon each other.

The powers of the Universe are *infinite*. So when you want things that are not your desires, and are not in line with those Universal powers, you create blockages that further separate you from them. You *want* the powers of the Universe in your corner. Why?

We want you to consider that the powers of the Universe are so very vast and powerful that they are capable of *anything*.

Indeed, we suggest you take the necessary time for this to sink in.

> *You have the powers of the Universe at your*
> *hands, and at your feet, so why would you*
> *bother to want things that are so very*
> *insignificant that they actually distract you*
> *from the riches of the Universe?*

Indeed, you do not. So you will want to move your attention away from wanting superfluous things and follow your bliss, for the Universe is designed to provide it for you.

The way you can take the way of spirit to the bank is simple: *trust*. That's all. Trust is the most important thing you can have, because it allows your essence to help you.

That's right: we want you to trust, as we've said over and over. We're not talking about a kind of "blind faith," but cultivating a deep trust in yourself and your personal connection with your essence.

Explore ways to speak with essence

There are a variety of ways to communicate with essence. Let's begin with a simple example. Imagine that you have a ball of string, and you take one end and tie a knot to anchor it to something that won't move. Then you pull your string tight and play a melody of your choice. You might play the simplest melody with one note, or you can extend or shorten the string to play other notes. The string will accommodate a variety of notes, and therefore, you can play any song you want within the range.

The trick is to know the range that is available to you and play the songs you desire. You can be assured that if you have become a "one note Johnny," plucking the same note to boring distraction, essence will urge you to expand your range and play a song that is more fitting of the divinity that lives in and through you.

So trust that there are ways to communicate with your essence through exciting new songs that beautifully reflect your way of spirit. For example, Rose speaks through another human being. Why, therefore, would you believe that you can't do exactly the same thing with your essence? You have the ability to do so. That's right, it's easy, for what you desire is to reconnect with your own sense of Godhood. Indeed, your essence is there to always assist, and you will find this process extremely valuable. Here's how we suggest you do this.

First; trust that you have the natural ability to tune directly into your essence in ways that are common. Your essence will be summoned by your prayers and in other intuitive, improvisational, and beautiful ways. Beauty speaks volumes about your Godhood, so trust that when you do beautiful, exquisite, deeply compassionate things, you will connect with as well as express your essence.

Then, find your own way to meditate. The meditation practice will guide you towards your essence in ways that will feel safe as well as immensely beautiful.[11]

Next, trust that you'll find your individual expression of Godhood. Some essences will speak to you in words like we do. Some will speak to you in deeds, some through your dreams, and some will speak to you through your animals, yes indeed! Animals speak with you all the time, you just have forgotten how to listen.

So you may hear voices, engage in healing, see visions, or spontaneously know things as you directly converse — yes, converse — with your own Personal God! Indeed, that's what they're here for!

They want to! Indeed, they desperately do. So help them to help you find your way of spirit by learning to trust, by meditating, and by finding your own individual means to converse with your essence. The families of intent information will help you do so.[12]

---

[11] See the Rest in Rose practice on page 192.
[12] See *Chapter 4: The Families of Intent.*

You can channel your Personal God

What we are suggesting is that you have the ability to channel. Our definition of *channeling* is *to bring internal information into your external world*. In this, the internal information is what you've come to understand as impressions, intuitions, impulses, words, voices, trusting in self, spontaneous knowing, etc. These are all valid ways to connect with essence.

We suggest you entice your essences by meditating for at least an hour a day in the mornings, if possible.

> *What better way to get the day started than a*
> *wonderful talk with God? Indeed none.*

We have a lot of experience with these matters. They are the best practices of your monastics, which is why we've assigned a rather monastic name to this special meditation: *Vespers*. [13]

These prayers began as the deeply spiritual rituals we are providing you, but became formal and somewhat rigid after being adopted by the Church. These ancient rites require a return to their original intention: to bring you into your own deep connection with—and expression of—your essence. So when you do your Vespers, you may feel a bit like a priest, monk, or nun, and we encourage this. Why not lay claim to the spiritual traditions that are your heritage, and spend part of each day speaking directly with the Universe? Indeed, when you don't, you deprive yourself of so much.

Moreover, you don't need to spend your meditation time in monasteries or temples, for your body is your temple. So

---

[13] See the Vespers practice on page 195.

we will also suggest that you take very good care of it! This is why your diet and exercise should be well balanced, as this will fulfill your way of spirit in bodily ways. Indeed, body, mind, and essence are all wonderful parts of your greater self, so trust that they are all very important. When you incorporate *all* of them you truly express your Godhood.

There is another part of your diet that we will suggest needs to be considered, and that is sex. Sex is one of the most beautiful expressions you can possibly have, and you need to do it responsibly. We so want you to connect with each other in beautiful ways that we don't know what to do, for you've forgotten in some ways how wonderful sex is. Trust yourself to find ways to pleasure yourself, to please others, and to fully experience your *senxuality*, because it helps you to connect with your essence. For Godhood is a *senxy* affair, indeed. We will explain.

Exploring your Godhood is senxual

You have been taught a most ridiculous thing: that divinity is stringently anti-sexual and you should therefore disavow all things senxual. This is so inaccurate we could cry, for your way of spirit includes senxuality in every way.

For instance, when you eat a strawberry, pet an animal, or immerse yourself in your wonderful world in ways in which you appreciate its smells, colors, flavors, and sensations, you get the most accurate sensations of Godhood. What more would you want?

Again, what you sometimes *want* is the problem. But when you senxually immerse yourself in your world, you experience God. Indeed, why would you want anything more than what you already have? Because you've been sold a bill of goods in regard to senxuality, so again let us assure you:

You are the most divine creatures when you fully entice yourself with the sensations of the world, and you can trust we will assist.

Your way of spirit is wonderful, it's senxual, it's pleasurable—it's a brisk walk in the morning, the smells you get when you roast a turkey, the wonderful expressions of joy in your foods, perfumes, and fine wines. When you believe that these things are bad, you diminish your enjoyment of the world's incredible beauty. *Don't.*

Try to remember that we're here in spirit, to egg you on and help you find your bliss in every way. So trust that when you enjoy a romp in the hay, a rolling meadow, or a wonderful, big laugh, that you are following your way of spirit in remarkable ways, so do so.

Therefore, you're right if you're thinking that connecting with your God is a senxual thing: it *is!* When you connect with your way of spirit, it will be most wonderfully senxy.

So do what you need to do to move into this phase of your lives, for it is indeed the most wonderful thing you can imagine as well as experience.

Key Ideas: Find Your Personal God

- You are much more than your ego, and have access to your own Personal God (essence).
- Your inspiration and innate spiritual wisdom are in the very genes in your bodies.
- Unfulfilled wants create hatred when you see them as blockages rather than the gentle nudging of spirit towards your true desires. When you learn to reconnect with spirit, you will no longer hate.

- Your ego self is the center of your Universe, not the entire Universe, which nurtures all things.
- When you want things that are not desires and not in line with infinite Universal powers, you create blockages that further separate you from them.
- Trust that you have a natural ability to communicate with your essence. Meditation can help. (See the Rest in Rose practice on page 192.)
- You have the ability to channel—to bring internal information into your external world—which is your individual expression of Godhood. (See *Chapter 4: The Families of Intent* to help you discover your unique way.)
- The Vespers practice is a meditation that will help you connect with and channel your Personal God. The morning is the best time to do Vespers, but they can be done any time of the day. (See the Vespers practice on page 195.)
- Your body is your temple, and it is important to take care of it through well balanced diet, exercise, and responsible sex.
- Your way of spirit includes senxuality. When you senxually immerse yourself in the world, you experience God.

Chapter 10: Trust in Your Dreams

T he way of spirit provides you with the greatest information you can imagine. All the information in the Universe is available right now within you, and can be accessed every night when you sleep. You may consider your dreams to be the antithesis of your waking state, but this is not the case. For in your dreams, you awaken to your essence self and hold the keys to your very existence.

Your dreams are nature's calling to you. Like music is to your ears, or art is to your eyes, your dreams are the inner language of your soul.

We suggest that you assess every dream you can, but pay attention to the clearer ones, as they are inner communications from your essence self that contain the most important information.

What more could you want from essence than experiences in dream space where you can do whatever you choose and know you could harm no one, not even yourself? For that's what dreams are, and while they are like your real life in some respects, they are uniquely designed to provide another way to communicate with essence that is perhaps the most interesting.

Your dreams are real

You have a gift for dreaming that seems most real. Some of the deepest and most important dreams you have are those that you would consider lucid, where you are awake and conscious in your dream state. Your waking life is like a lucid dream, but also not like it, due to the persistence of time. Your dream lives are always subject to change in a moment's notice. They allow you to explore scenarios that you may incorporate into your waking reality to help you perform in the world in ways that bring you bliss.

Your dream lives provide a similar way to look at your physical lives—and we mean deliberately to say *lives*—because that's why you dream as well. You dream to remember that you have many focuses of attention—or lifetimes, although you now are aware this is a misnomer.

Your current focus—your life—is your essence's way of expressing itself through you in your reality, just as your essence does for every one of your focuses of attention in other realities simultaneously.

In this, your focuses are also you, but they exist in both real time and history, past as well as future. So your history books are always being recreated based on probable realities that would be considered probable pasts, and your futures are dynamically changing to accommodate reality's needs to change as well, creating probable futures.

Your reality is your reality, but only in your present sense. Everything else is in a state of probabilities that includes your essence and many others who are establishing multiple timeframes, dimensions, probable selves, and endless experiences for you and others. Your dreams ensure you are aware of other focuses outside of your own waking life so that you may incorporate their experiences into your knowledge and vice versa. So in essence, you are—amazingly—providing yourself stories that you can learn from when you examine your dreams.

Every dream has value, especially the scary ones

You may be afraid to examine your dreams because sometimes you have terrible ones that make you afraid, but there is a way to find peace in this. For your dreams are your experiences, and you'll find as many horrors there as beauty, and in this, your dreams will not tell you lies. So when you are afraid of your dreams, it is because you have forgotten that you are only tapping into a variety of dimensions and timeframes, and the horrors are what you are there to discover so you will make different choices to shape your present reality.

Your essence always provides you with your best and most precious dreams, and these include even the scary ones. You know why you fear your dreams: you don't want that to happen to you. And you may have predicted what we are going to say next: you fear them because you have not yet accepted that you *are* them.

Your dreams tell you of the natural progression of your lives, and how you can have both your beautiful lives as well as those that you may not feel are beautiful because they are the ones in which you learn things in difficult ways. Your dreams represent the things you know about in other ways, too.

In your interpretations, you sometimes
miss the point: that you are the monsters,
that you are the angels, and that you are
the multitudinous essences that you are,
in your world and beyond it.

And your dreams provide guidance as to how you can be
at peace in your world, even in your scary dreams, for these
help you to become who we know you are: your essence self.

In this, what more important thing is there to do than
sleep, perchance to dream? Indeed, you cannot go without
sleep for as long as you can without food or water. Sleeping
and dreaming are more important than even those. Why?
Because they are your way of deeply connecting with essence.
So when you dream, you ensure you are in step with your
Personal God—your essence—and lovingly provide yourself
with guidance should you choose to examine them.

What more could you want than your essences telling you
what you need to do in your days? Indeed, you will tell
yourself things to watch out for, things to avoid, and
prophecies, even, at times.

And when you are suggesting to yourself that you won't
remember your dreams, remember that you already know
your dreams, you just don't remember the details. Your
dreams are as much a part of you as anything—even your skin
on your bodies—so your dreams will always be close to you
and help you realize them. And in this, probabilities will
occur.

As we've said, probabilities are the means in which life
happens. They are your way of sensing your future as well as
your past. Therefore, know that the probabilities in your life
are that: probabilities.

There is no set course for your life. You create your
course, and your dreams provide you keys to finding
your greatest, most beautiful paths to take.

Daydreams help you find and live your desires

When you consider your dreams, also consider your daydreams as keys to determining your desires. The way to do this is simply to daydream, then look at the daydreams differently.

Say you are daydreaming about the future probabilities around baseball. What will it look like in fifty years? You may have more than one league, one that uses performance-enhancing drugs, for example. Perhaps you would like to have something to do with this in one way or another. You might sense how your desires could play into the scenario, then find out what you would need to do that. Here's how.

When you daydream, you tell yourself what you want.
When you tell yourself what you want, you allow
probable selves to tell you what you desire, for it's in
your desires that you really, truly find your bliss.

Say your probable selves tell you that you don't want to get into baseball, and that your daydream was more about not allowing the performance enhancing drugs to be provided to sports players of any age. That would be a way, perhaps, to nurture children by first presenting the idea to yourself that children shouldn't use drugs such as steroids. Do you follow? You would need to settle upon what it would be about that daydream that gets you going, that gets your heart pounding, and your willingness to do something in your world really steaming along. And why? Because it is your *desire*. That is what you needed to find out, and you did this through a simple daydream.

Here's another example. Say you wanted to refine your way of doing some things, like water skiing. Say you found, in your daydream, a way to fly while water skiing that has not been done before. Do you want to fly on water skis? Maybe not. Maybe you just want the feeling of flying on water skis. Why would you want this? Perhaps you're perfecting another technique for flying on air and you are getting a sense of how that would work by situating your problem in the context of water. Why wouldn't this work? It would, and it's been done already.

So when you are daydreaming, try to provide yourself with fantasies in which you would like to move into your world in wondrous ways, then tell your daydream "thank you," for it is your communication with essence.

Essence knows what you are seeking and will do everything in its power to tell you.

Now, back you go to work and you have these great daydreams in your mind. What do you do? You find ways to incorporate them into your work, but perhaps not all at once. You will need to find ways to make moves in your life to allow you the kind of roles that will allow you to quickly incorporate your daydreams into your lives, and your essences will help you.

For now, keep in mind that this is entirely possible, as well as probable, for *reading this book right now is your way of telling yourself that this is a most probable probability.* Your work in the world is in every way important to us, so consider your daydreams important tools for you to more fully embrace your *total* lives, not just your wonderful daydreamy lives. For your lives are *your lives*, and you in no way are expected to partition off yourself in ways you've been doing for so very long.

So look forward to a beautifully integrated dream life in your waking life, for knowing how to do this is important and practical as you find more ways to incorporate your essence into your every moment.

You can access the wisdom of the Universe

We'll allow just a bit more about dreams. Your wanting to accept and invite your dreams is important, and we mean even the scary things that you may discover there. For in some ways, you are your dreams and your dreams are you. And your essence is always your dreams, too. We'll explain.

When you realize how much your essence will help you when you allow it, you will get a greater idea of how very vast it is, and you are.

In your way of spirit, you will avail yourself of the wisdom of the Universe, as your essence has your wisdom and every bit of wisdom ever created in its reach. And you, in every way, have access to it, too. But you don't realize that until you ask for it.

Prayer is one way to do this, for realizing prayer is your way of defining your wants, needs, and desires while also allowing your essence to speak back. It is what you do naturally in every breath when you hope for the best outcomes for yourself and the world. When you pray in the morning for your essence to come through you in your days, and in your evenings before you sleep to instill in yourself your needs and enable yourself to prioritize, you get the best of all possible worlds. For your dreams will satisfy your prayers in ways that you will sense is only miraculous. And here's why.

As we said, when you dream, you realize how very vast you are as essence. You as essence have a vast number of focuses in your reality and in other dimensions as well. When you dream, you can visit any of them, and your focus helps you direct yourself to your needs area, in a sense. So if you are feeling blue, you may want to allow yourself a visit to a place of joy that you as essence experience. And when you are feeling—as you sometimes do—unkind, perhaps you will find ways to resolve your hatred, for you have many focuses in which you suffer and cause suffering, too.[14]

So you have the benefit of viewing and experiencing a vast many focuses of attention that you'd consider helpful. When you consider that yours is one of many focuses that are happening at once, you can begin to appreciate the vastness of you as essence. And when you do, consider that your intent is a very important part of this.

Consciousness provides infinite experience

As we've said, your belonging-to intent is your essence's theme of sorts for its many focuses of attention, and in this, you will experience a sort of harmonic with all of your focuses as long as you are experiencing your own essence. Some of these experiences may have greater resonance than others. When you have an experience that does not seem harmonic, you may be experiencing a focus that is not of your own essence. The reason this is a valuable experience is because it will allow you to see across a vast expanse of Selfhood. In other words: ultimately, you are All That Is. We will explain.

---

[14] See the Evening Prayers practice on page 197.

There is no experience that you
cannot have in Consciousness.

Your essence expresses itself as a "thematic poet" of conscious intention, and each lifetime is a very important part of this expression. So when you get discouraged about things, remember that you are an extremely important part of All That Is, so much so that All That Is encourages you to speak to Itself all the time. And why not? We, as essence, are intermediaries for All That Is, and you are an aspect of All Of That. So really let this sink in.

You are a very important part of the Universe, and
your life is important to all of us, as we need you,
we need your experiences, and we need your
wonderful, beautiful creations.

In other words, you are the eyes, ears, and lips of God Itself, and why would you not provide yourself the assurances you need to be Gods in your world? Indeed, you would not want to portion yourself off as you have been and cause yourself pain. In some ways, this provides experience, but you are reading this book now and know that this is no longer necessary.

So allow essence to provide the best information you need, and sleep in peace knowing that *you are not only eternal—you are in every way loved.* And you don't need to worry about any ogres or boogey men. You *are* them. You are your providers of pain, you are your providers of joy, and remembering this is an important part of your spiritual journey. So when you find yourself remembering that you are Joan of Arc, remember you are also the bowery slummer with no shoes and who has no remembrance of his hat.

*For you are part of All That Is, and you have access to
the All Knowing: you just have forgotten.*

Now is when you will remember. This is why you chose
this book: to help you remember what you chose—in
essence—to forget. The forgetting enabled you to explore
areas of experience that you would not otherwise, in order to
benefit yourself and many others. Why else would you be
remembering Yourself to yourself? Indeed, so you may
expand your notions of reality and, in doing so, help your
world, help your brothers and sisters, and help your
creatures.

But first, you will need to help yourself. And the way you
might begin is to examine what happens when you allow your
shadow self to get in the way.

Key Ideas: Trust in Your Dreams

- Dreams are inner communications from your essence
  that allow you to access all the information in the
  Universe.
- Dreams are more critical to your physical health than
  food or water.
- Dreams help you try out probable scenarios and find the
  most fulfilling paths to take.
- Your scary dreams help you remember the vastness of
  your essence.
- Essence tells you in your dreams things that you want to
  watch out for, things to avoid, and, at times, prophecies.
- Daydreams help you discover your wants. Examining
  those, with the help of probable selves, helps you find
  and live your desires.

- Prayer helps you define and prioritize your needs in ways that help essence bring you the information you need. (See the Evening Prayers practice on page 197.)

- There is no experience that you cannot have in consciousness.

- You are a very important part of the Universe. Your life, experiences and creations are needed. You are the eyes, ears, and lips of God Itself.

- You can sleep in peace knowing that you are eternal and in every way loved.

Chapter 11: The Shadow

There are many ways to tell things about a person. One is to pay attention to how he thinks, acts, or speaks. Another is to pay attention to what he complains about, for in this, you'll be provided clues to his shadow and yours. Your shadow will often get in your way and create all sorts of obstacles. Learning to notice and address it will speed you along your way of spirit so well that you'll wonder why you never noticed it before.

The shadow is a necessary aspect of self that brings
focus to thoughts and actions that conflict with your
desires so that you may address them.

Your shadow expresses itself when you find yourself wanting what you don't really desire, and become frustrated when you don't get it. It is that part of you that accommodates your fears and wants, when in fact you need to look more deeply within yourself and find ways to align your intent and desires. You can think of your shadow as what happens when you don't align correctly with the sun of your Personal God, who only wants you to be happy. Indeed, your shadow is what happens when you get in your own way.

Your shadow is a part of you that *inflates* and *deflates* others. *Shadow inflation* happens when you think that you can't get what you want and you project onto others who seem to have the power to do so. In this way, you project your own lack of power onto someone else who seems more powerful than you. *Shadow deflation* happens when you project onto others that they are bad, flawed, or lacking in some way. In this case, you project your dislike of *your own* flaws and lacks onto another. That's right: you recognize the flaws but misidentify them as belonging to someone else.

Both are related in the same way: they impose on *others* to express *your* desires, when *you* have the power all along.

When you allow your shadow to be in charge, you
immediately invalidate your own power.

Your shadow can make you aware of your desires

Making your shadow smaller is the key to helping you dominate it, for your bigness is in essence, not ego. You can think of yourself as an immense spirit who will not block your sunlight, but your ego sometimes will. To entice your ego to become smaller in this way will both serve your ego and place it in direct alignment with your desires.

In this, we suggest you think of yourself as very small. We will suggest you "get small," as your comedian Steve Martin suggested so many years ago. Get small to allow your big egos to rest in the knowledge they are doing a great job and don't need to work so hard and make yourself bigger than you need to be. In this, you will allow a smaller footprint and more deeply realize the sunshine in your heart and soul.

What do you desire from life? You desire serenity, peace, and harmony. Why don't you always have it? Because your ego wants things you don't truly desire, and when it does, the shadow will be there to support the ego in obtaining those things, however ill-suited for you they are.

Ultimately, your shadow only wants to make you aware of what you desire, and does it in ways that are easy to spot. In this, you can consider your shadow to be a helpful part of your physical reality, as long as you notice what it—*you*—are really doing and work to correct its—*your*—ways as soon as possible. You can think of your shadow as a fair weather friend who makes clouds in your life and then leaves when it starts to rain. The shadowy clouds fly in from areas of consciousness that you need to allow into the sunshine so you can identify why you are raining on yourself and your life.

Here's an example. Say you want to have a party, but you don't know what to do about the decorations. The party is a good, wonderful thing, and your shadow says, "I think you'll want to get better decorations than Suzy had at *her* party. She isn't as good as you, so she shouldn't be allowed to have better decorations." So your shadow tells you that you're better than someone, and also says you'll be a better person by having better decorations.

Although this may sound like a very sweet and simple explanation that you wouldn't do in a million years, you would be incorrect: you do this all the time, you just don't notice it. Indeed, why would you? You've been taught that the way you need to live is to outdo and overdo everything in ways that are extremely superficial. So yes, trust that you do this.

You must notice and manage your shadow

You can notice your shadow at work when you don't feel that you're doing well enough. You may feel intensely insecure. You may not even consider that the least important thing about your party is the decorations. You only *think* that you'll be happy when you try to overdo and outdo. Indeed, you *won't*: you'll be *less* happy because you'll compare yourself to someone else in hopes that you'll feel like a bigger, better individual. You sentence yourself to a life of trying to do things to make you feel *better* that only make you feel *worse*.

> *Would you do this if you were allowing your*
> *greatness to shine in other ways?*
> *No, you wouldn't.*

In this, you need to notice when your shadow is at work. Your shadow *wants* you to notice, and does so in a big way. It will say, "You're not getting *those* decorations, are you? They're awful! They'll hate them!" If you don't notice the shadow at work, you will get yourself so wrapped around your axle that you won't want to do anything. You will take the joy right out of the event. Indeed, you always want the best for yourself, and you'll do well to continue. But the way we want you to think of this is that you'll do better when you allow yourself to trust your choices and be damned with everything else.

That may sound strict and harsh, but why wouldn't you just do what you want as long as you didn't hurt anyone? Indeed, do you see the harm you inflict on yourself when you get wrapped upon your axles in regard to your shadow? Indeed, you do. So you need learn to recognize that when you feel bad, you have always invoked your shadow—*always!* For there's never any reason to feel bad—*never!* Therefore, it's always part of your shadow work to *notice* when you feel bad and address the issues that are causing it.

What to do when you feel bad

Here is what we suggest the next time you notice yourself feeling bad. Take a deep breath and for a moment examine what's really bothering you. Is it the things *others* are doing? No it isn't. Is it the things *you're* doing? Yes it is. And what can you do to help yourself to *not* do those things? You begin by *trusting self*. And why wouldn't you trust yourself? Because you don't believe you are powerful enough, or deserving enough, to have what you truly desire.

Your ego teams with your shadow to get things you don't really want or need because you don't believe deep down that you can have what you desire. So you end up wanting things that you don't need or desire, then project your shadow onto others thinking they are the cause of your inability to have what you desire, and they never have anything to do with it — *never!*

Then you suggest to yourself even more loudly than before that you will never get what you *desire*, when in reality, you were only trying to get what you *wanted*. This creates a cycle of suffering that you would do well to break.

Alternately, you often absorb people's infirmities, obsessions, guilt, and other negative emotions. When you try to get past that, you find that they are only responding to their shadows.

So you can trust that if Suzy — if she's anyone who matters, and if the people at your parties are anyone who matters — will criticize you for your party decorations, that they can go to hell, or to put it more accurately, stay there, for that's exactly where they are. They are in the hell of their shadows, and their egos are in such pain that they don't know what to do. They may desire health, or love, or peace of mind, but they don't have it, and don't know how to get it. This forms a cycle of suffering, the results of which are never satisfying and create more pain than you might even imagine.

So you must learn to let go of your unnecessary wants and trust that what you truly desire is to have a party that's really wonderful in spite of your lousy decorations. Who cares? Indeed, not us. We love ugly party decorations and think they're the best ones, in some respects. Because the best parties are those with the best of friends, the best of foods, the best of drinks, and the best times that you could imagine.

Indeed, we're not casting dispersions on party decorations, they are becoming to you in ways that are artful. But we want to really get the message across to you.

> *The decorations are more than just a metaphor*
> *for your shadow play: they are a metaphor for*
> *your lives in your consumerist society.*

So trust that the decorations, indeed, exist on many levels.

Essence will tell you what your shadow is blocking

Your ego is a beautiful and necessary element in your psychological makeup. We are not suggesting for a moment that your ego is bad, it just often gets in the way of what you desire.

To take yourself out of yourself is the point: the ego wants to call all the shots, but it doesn't. We do. Essence, ultimately, calls the shots. Your ego takes the best approaches it knows of, but it doesn't know everything. We do. That's right. Your essence knows, well, almost everything you can imagine and then some.

Your ego can't even conceive everything that's possible. So why would you trust it with all your decisions? When you allow your shadow to beguile your ego into doing certain things, you're only scratching the surface of your many choices and probabilities, which are truly vast and beyond your imagination. But you can tune into them, and the way you do this is to

Pay attention to what your shadow is getting in the way of. In this, the beautiful treasure lies.

Now, when we last left our heroine, she wanted some party decorations. Her ego said that she had to get better ones than Suzy, because Suzy's party had been profoundly beautiful. That's why our heroine is so afraid to proceed, for how can she best Suzy in the decoration department? Indeed, maybe she can't. So she tries and tries, but to no avail, and she gets scared that no one will enjoy her party. But what if she were to turn her attention to herself and trust that her decorations will indeed make for a beautiful party no matter what happened at Suzy's party? That is the real idea behind the whole exercise.

Indeed, our heroine is so afraid to make incorrect decisions that she immerses herself in everything but her real desire: to have a wonderful party. As a result, she fails to see that she would be better off to trust herself to have a nice party. In this, the expression "you get what you concentrate on" becomes realized, and she creates that very thing—a terrible party. And she does this is by ignoring her shadow, rather than noticing it and realizing what her shadow was really telling her to address: it's the party, not the decorations.

Who doesn't do this a thousand times a day in some way? Indeed you *all* do, so you'd do well to embrace the lessons that your shadow points out to you and learn to address the things you notice. In doing so, you will allow the fulfillment of your desires.

Now, let's explore the deflation of others a bit further, and how you sometimes deflate the choices of others, as well as the individuals themselves.

Others need you to *not* deflate their choices

When you judge the choices that others make in ways that create suffering, only sontering your Personal God will help you.[15] Sontering provides you the best means to counter the willingness to make shadow judgments and deflate the choices others make. The benefits of the sontering practice become clearer when you do it, for you will discover that the individuals in your life are as needy as you are at times, and you will find less need to deflate their choices. They will find you to be a wonderful friend, for you will open like a flower in ways that you'll find extremely satisfying.

So make sure that when you deflate someone and their choices, that they need you to be a friend in the truest sense. For as surely as they want in their lives only the people who appreciate them, they will find you in beautiful ways.

For finding the beauty in their choices is the point — not deflating them — and to feel truly happy for others provides the deepest joy and purpose you can imagine.

So when you deflate someone or their choices, remember *they need you to not do that.* We will say more about this later.

---

[15] See the Sonter (Breathe in Essence) practice on page 191.

Let's continue with a discussion about shadow inflation, as this offers another crucial way to become happy and healthy, and yet is often the most invisible of the two.

You *shadow inflate* those you want to be

Shadow inflation happens when you overstate a person's importance so much that you become blind to their very human flaws. It may happen when you find a person whom you idealize—like the president of your country, the head of a movie studio, an actor whom you consider "hot"—or find yourself noticing how wonderful someone is. Indeed, they may be most wonderful, but you inflate them in ways in which you consider yourself to be less than they are. For they would be doing no harm by you in any way, but you would be doing yourself harm by only seeing their value, not the human, flawed side.

Indeed, by flawed we mean according to the definition we've already provided: the things that have not been addressed—the fears, the lack of compassion, the anxieties. The flaws are your perceived wrongs about yourself as well as others that are not wrongs in a real sense, only in your perceptions. Certainly we want you to become better people—trust that we do—but you don't need to consider yourself flawed, in any way, from birth, only in your perceptions about yourself.

Take for example people in your movies. They may have great abilities, great skills in gaining fame, and they may be beautiful, but they are *not* perfect. When you find a person who is perfect, let us know, because we essences would love to see them! The way you can consider this to be true is to remember that they are people just like you. They have their flaws, in the way we've defined them previously, the things that they have not addressed—their fears and anxieties. And when they fear, they hurt just like you. So try to be considerate of individuals in your movies, in your world, and in your provision of celebrity, because they hurt like you do.

Why do you want to take them down? Because you project *your* fears of not being good enough onto *them*, then you want to make them suffer. In this, you'd be projecting your shadow of deflation, and the two are in many ways the same. In the first scenario, you *inflate* their choices by believing they *are* better than you, or even perfect, and in the second, you *deflate* their choices by believing they *should be*. You expect too much, then are disappointed when you find they are only human, and hurting, as you are.

> *You shadow inflate those you want to be,*
> *and shadow deflate those you do not.*

The way you project your shadow of inflation onto individuals will make you crazy, because you can't have everything they have, nor do you desire it. However, there are things that people do that you'd do well to emulate, and when you project the shadow of inflation, you can remind yourself of why you are doing that.

We will explain more a bit later, but for now, keep in mind that individuals who aspire to do great things do so without the need for projecting shadow, but in identifying the gifts and abilities that others have that they can aspire to.

The concept of *ego inflation* relates to shadow inflation, for your egos want to think they're perfect, and you support this notion when you project onto someone your own shadow inflation. In this, ego inflation and shadow inflation work exactly the same way to repel the goodness about you by allowing you to only *think* you're doing right. These are things that involve preening, self-aggrandizement, finding only superficial friends, and finding *things* more important than *people*.

In this, your way of spirit is blocked and you're not the happiest person you can be in spite of your so-called wonderful life. What you will find is an emptiness in spirit, and this is not preferred. It is a choice, indeed, and one that has some value in the Youniverse. But you'll find it to be a treacherous path in many ways, as you'll find things that initially excite you, but eventually you'll see as the shallow expressions they are.

So trust that we're not saying this path is bad—it's only short—and you'll find that you'll want to move on to get the whole world in your hands, not just the things that provide the appearance of shiny perfection. In this, your ego inflation can affect you in ways that would be considered shadow inflation.

The ego is an important supporting player

The way you can think of your ego is as a supporting player, not the main player. Your essence self is the main player, and you can trust us on this one. You'll find that your ego will rebel at this, and may be doing so as you read this, and this is its job: to rebel, in some ways, against spirit. This is the hardest thing to explain, but we'll say that your intuition is correct in wanting the full story, for it's an important one.

The ego will seek satisfaction on a limited scale, because that is what the ego has learned. So your ego is acting from a lower stage of development that wants only what it has learned so far. It's as if you take a third grader and put him into fourth grade. What does he know? The ways of being a third grader. Is there anything wrong with this? Absolutely not, he's only doing what he's learned. So moving from one coat room to another may be a difficult or simple thing, depending on the degree of complexity.

This is what you do in everyday life: you focus on what you know, and what more can you do? Exactly. You can call on your essence to assist you in what you *don't* know, as well as what you *need to* know. And in this, you'll find there's a lot you don't know, including ways in which you can achieve more than your ego knows how.

Your essence will show you things you'll find extremely satisfying, like possible ways to solve problems that you didn't notice before, prophetic ways to look at options, or informative ways to look into people's minds and souls. We suggest you do this already, you just don't realize it, and that

By allowing your shadow to point out where your ego
is getting in your way, you'll allow the ego to relax
and enjoy the ride in ways it will find wonderful.

So let your ego rest, and be assured that it will be most happy to do that. For it will find a friend in your essence, as we are constantly helping to find ways it may assist, and indeed, that's the ego's job. It's a wonderful team of selves you're creating in your reality, so trust that your ego, shadow, and essence selves are fine, you just need to allow them to get in tune with each other.

How you'll find that ego *inflation*, therefore, is similar to and often the same as the ego *deflation*, is that your ego will *inflate* when it thinks that it *does* know all the answers, and will *deflate* when it thinks that it *doesn't*. So the ego needs to be in check with essence to ensure the shadow doesn't intrude. Sometimes your ego will be in check, but you won't trust that your choices will be sound. In this, you need to trust your essence self and your choices, which we've told you about.

Ego inflation and shadow inflation

Let us continue with the discussion about ego inflation and shadow inflation. The shadow wants the trust of your ego, so it will assure the ego that it has its best interests in mind. The ego, wanting to help you, will sometimes not notice it is being challenged and therefore will interest itself in the shadow's suggestions. In this, the ego will fail you.

For example, would you offer a blind dog a bone to chew on? Yes, you would, if you were helping the doggy. And would you take off the butcher's wrappings before you do? That would be the kind thing to do, correct? Your essence would suggest you do so. The ego self may say, "Well, that's not on my schedule, so the dog can fend for himself." We suggest this would cause you pain—in some small way, perhaps—knowing that you could have been kinder and you weren't.

This is an example of ego inflation getting in the way. The ego wants only what it wants and will not allow your essence to influence. And so you have pain. As much as you want to ignore the pain, you do indeed have it. So trust us on this one and allow us to continue to discuss the how ego inflation is related to shadow inflation.

The shadow comes in to tell you that you didn't do anything wrong. You're a very important person who doesn't have time to help a blind dog. After all, you gave him a bone, didn't you? We suggest your ego will tell itself it's satisfied and move on. Then it will attach itself to some other wonderful individual whom you will try to emulate, get into the pants of, scream at on the television, lie to when you feel they may provide a promotion at your job, or feel insecure around, for this is what you do.

You continue to attach yourself to expectations of how you're supposed to be, and in this, you project your shadow of inflation. In this, you ignore your way of spirit, for your ego will only rely on what it knows already, and it knows that it wants to emulate certain people it thinks it's supposed to, so it does. And when it does—*watch out*—for this causes more misery than you could ever imagine.

The shadow is a big topic that we want to tell you more about, so stay tuned, and we will take it up in the next chapter, *How to Manage Your Shadow.*

Key Ideas: The Shadow

- Your *shadow* is a necessary aspect of self that brings focus to thoughts and actions that conflict with your desires so that you may address them.

- *Shadow inflation* happens when you think that you can't get what you want and project onto others who seem to have the power to do so.

- *Shadow deflation* happens when you project your dislike of *your own* flaws and lacks onto another.

- Both shadow inflation and deflation invalidate your own power and perpetuate suffering.

- Your shadow can be a helpful part of your physical reality as long as you notice what it—*you*—are really doing and work to correct its—*your*—ways as soon as possible.

- Sontering—breathing in essence—is the best way to counter the willingness to make shadow judgments. (See the Sonter—Breathe in Essence practice on page 191.)

- *Ego inflation* and shadow inflation work together by allowing you to only think you're doing right.
- Ego inflation happens when your ego thinks it knows all the answers, and *ego deflation* happens when it thinks it doesn't.
- When you pay attention to what your shadow is getting in the way of, you will discover your desires.
- Your ego can help only as much as it knows how. Essence assists in what you don't know, but need to know.
- When you learn to trust your essence and allow your shadow to point out what your ego is getting in your way, you'll allow your ego self to relax and enjoy the ride.

Chapter 12: How to Manage Your Shadow

A s we've said, the shadow is what happens when you get in the way of your own sunshine. This happens when you only get to know yourself at the ego level, find fault with yourself in ways that are unhealthy, provide yourself excuses for harmful behaviors, and try to rid your fears and doubts by unloading on others, which of course never works.

Remember that you are inherently good

The way you can distinguish between shadow projections of inflation and deflation is to ask yourself, are they overly "good" or overly "bad" towards another? In this, you can consider them both "bad" in the sense that they are unhealthy. You can think of them as *unhealthy*—not *bad*—for *you* are not bad, only hurting.

You can look to your upbringing and find many ways—perhaps more than you realize—that you've been led to believe that you're bad when indeed you're not. Again, you're not flawed from birth and you're not lacking grace—you *always* have grace and you always are forgiven, no matter what you do. You don't *want* to do bad things—not because someone tells you to, but—because you're inherently good, and to do bad things isn't like you.

When you do things that would be considered violations, you find pain, you find hell, and you find joylessness in your days. And when you feel that way, you project onto the world how you feel, and that is lousy.

So what do you do? You find fault with others, you find fault with the world, when the world is exactly the same as you in every way: it's hurting, too.

In this, you project shadow to take your mind off your deepest selves and project onto the world what you find troubling in yourself. The shadow buys into the view that you are *not* perfectly imperfect, that you have no compassion for the world, that you must force your ways on others, and that you must often treat other people—and yourself—badly.

The shadow never goes away because it is needed for your growth, for you are learning in some ways, and in other ways you're already perfect. This sounds a bit Zen, and it is. But don't think for a moment that you were sent to the planet to let your shadow rule it, for that is not your path, it is never anyone's path. Sometimes the path is chosen, but you'll do well to not fight fire with fire, and instead, to fight fire with love and compassion. In this, you must provide yourself as much love and compassion as possible.

It is in truly loving yourself that you'll get most comfort, and in this, you'll manage your shadow.

Find your sense of inner beauty

Your way of spirit is the way of finding *peace* in your world, not *shadow*. You can provide this for yourself by finding your most beautiful sense of yourself and feel as great as possible, always. If you're not feeling great, you're not following your way of spirit.

You'll find that the contrary self will help you be in your world—warts and all—and let go of your expectations about how you, and life, should be. Trust that your life is exactly as it should be. Your ego may feel small in such a vast Universe, for you are, indeed, both large and small. But for now, the focus is on your small ways of spirit, and your contrary self will always assist.

Next, trust your essence to help whenever you need it. For you are connected to All That Is, and It is only Good. You'll do well to forgive yourself and take a breath every now and then to thank yourself for the beautiful things you have. And when you do, you'll find yourself basking in the glow of your love and the love of the Universe. The way you can trust that is in your heart: look inside your heart and you'll find peace. That's all you need to do, and your shadow will find other ways to interest you, by pointing out your flaws in ways that you can consider helpful.

Address your beliefs

The way you can think of your flaws is as ways you don't love yourself yet, based upon incorrect beliefs you've been raised with. Your flaws *want* to get out of the way, so you need to *let* them. The way to do this is to notice a shadow projection, identify the belief causing it, define how you can address it, and then do so. It's a simple exercise that you can call *IDEA... Identify, Define, and Effortlessly Address your beliefs.*[16]

---

[16] For a condensed version of the Identify, Define, and Effortlessly Address your beliefs (IDEA) practice, see page 193.

When you notice your shadow pop up, say, when someone tells you something that aggravates you, look inside yourself to sonter—breathe in your essence self—to *identify* what the issue is *in you*.[17] This is a way to find flaws you haven't addressed yet, such as wanting things you don't really desire, wanting the best for yourself but no one else, finding fault with the way you look, etc.

Then you *define* how to address the problem. You might choose to explore and identify you true desires, assist others in ways that you find satisfying, too, find ways to be at peace with your looks, and myriad other ways to define your next actions to *effortlessly address your beliefs*. In this, you'll find out how to get the hell out of your way: addressing your limiting beliefs will put you into the light of your own being.

Your beliefs will get you in and out of your predicaments in astonishing ways.

> *Your beliefs, in every way, create your*
> *reality, along with your effortless*
> *allowance of spirit.*

In this, your beliefs sometimes block your natural inclination to be happy, spiritual people. In this, you'll block your energetic provision of spirit in ways that can be effortlessly removed once you identify and address the beliefs. The idea isn't to remove the beliefs, only to sort them out to help you figure out how to get happy.

So you can think of effortlessness not as the way you would address your issues, as these will take effort, but as your natural advantage as spiritual individuals, for the effortlessness is *in spirit*, not in your human terms. So you seek effortlessness, but you will not always get it.

---

[17] See the Sonter (Breathe in Essence) practice on page 191.

That's why you need to realize your spiritual natures, so you can help yourself find easier ways to live, not harder. The spiritual path isn't hard—it's easy—but the way you get there can be hard. Doing your intensely personal IDEA practice is the way to allow a more effortless spiritual path.

The IDEA practice: an example

So let's say someone has made an unkind comment about your looks. You first need to access alternative views of the situation.[18] These will be things that sound simple, but you'd be surprised how many times you overlook the many options you have in thinking about things.

You may consider that the person may have meant to be helpful, and that you really could take better care of yourself and how you look. You may consider that the person is not one to talk, and is projecting their own shadow at you. You may consider that the person was joking, but it came across as mean. You may consider that the person has made several mean remarks like this, and may need to be told that their comments are hurtful to you. Perhaps they may not be as good a friend as you thought, and you may discover that you need better friends. Or you may have reason to tell someone else they need to make more of an effort with the way groom themselves, and you find the person's lack of subtlety a means to define and address how you might go about *not* doing so. Any of these scenarios would provide potential ways to define and address the beliefs causing the problem.

Let's say that in your consideration of all these alternatives, you identify an issue as your own insecurity about your beauty, or perceived lack of it. Now it is time to define how to address it.

---

[18] See the Access Alternatives practice on page 187.

Consider the simplest things, like, do you really want to be that beautiful? Because you may be excited to learn that being beautiful isn't all it's cracked up to be. You may find that you don't want to be the most beautiful person alive. You'd do well to say to yourself, "You know, I'm not a bad-looking person one bit. In fact, I'm rather attractive in my own way, and I wouldn't necessarily want to be as beautiful as she is because I'm uniquely myself and there's no one else quite like me."

And that would be true, and that would be spiritual, and that would excellently provide you the basics for spiritual ways:

> *In accepting yourself, you accept the many*
> *millions of potentialities in your world and drop*
> *your expectations and worries about things*
> *needing to be certain ways.*

You would see that everything in your world has pluses and minuses, and in finding the minuses in the pluses and the pluses in the minuses, you embrace the world in ways that will be considered truly joyous.

For joy isn't the absence of suffering—it's the absence of ego—and in this, you get swept towards heaven in your understanding that suffering is inherent to life to help you find your joy. You'll be glad you are exactly how you are. You'll get a sense of deep appreciation for who you are in astounding ways. So when you define the problem, you get to peek into alternate ways to get happy by viewing potentialities that you'll experience when you effortlessly address your issues.

In this, you'll effortlessly allow the flow of spirit into your bodies and minds in healing ways, and your shadow will be the one to assist. But don't feel that the shadow is your best friend, your enemy, or your best counsel: it isn't. It is an advisor you would do well to keep closer to you than anyone else so you can keep an eye on it.

Your shadow is like a spy who knows no boundaries because it has been banished from your ego's territory for representing parts of you that you consider unacceptable or unworthy. It sees more than your ego can see and gives you important information, *but don't follow its advice,* for it will be based on your fears and doubts, and will thwart your plans for happiness. Your ego self will want to follow your shadow's advice, but your essence will tell you otherwise, *and this is where the treasure lies.*

> *In addressing to the issues it points towards, you will find ways to turn what the shadow gives you into gold: the realization of your deepest desires.*

How addressing beliefs saved the party

Let's go back to our party scenario. Our heroine, it turns out, had a terrible time at her party. She hadn't focused on her needs or desires to have a fun party, but instead had taken the advice of her shadow about besting Suzy with the decorations. She felt she'd failed herself and her friends.

But then she found a way to feel better, and it wasn't by listening to her shadow again, who suggested she blame Suzy and everyone else for her misery. Instead, she recognized that the problem was squarely *hers.*

She *identified* the problem: she had been overly concerned about the decorations. Why had they been so important? She accessed many alternatives.

Did she *really* want to outdo Suzy? Was there an unspoken competition she'd been unaware of? Didn't she trust that the other aspects of the party would be satisfying? Were the shiny decorations so engaging that she temporarily lost her judgment? She *had* been quite taken with the colors and the patterns and the themes of all the many decorations in a way she'd not noticed before.

After much soul searching, she *defined* the problem: she needed to express herself in ways that she hadn't considered. She realized there were aspects to the decorating that she'd desired to express but had not allowed herself. The tightening of energy around the decorations pointed towards a visual arts practice she had been longing for.

She then *effortlessly addressed* to the problem. She decorated her room in ways she found beautiful. She decorated her friends' rooms. She went into the business of party decorations and earned some cash on the side. Eventually, she took courses in art and interior design that potentiated a livelihood that brought her bliss.

Manage your shadow to realize your desires

The party pooped by anyone's estimation, yet our heroine found a way to make the party pop when she realized she was missing out on something she desperately desired. She learned to use her shadow to her advantage. She also learned the importance of decoration, not necessarily as a primary means to have a good party, but as a calling to her life's intent.

By buying into the shadow's suggestions about the decorations, our heroine may have lost the battle, but when she realized how important decorating was to her, the prize was hers to claim. This was potentiated by her doing the work she needed to find her way of spirit again, the result of managing her shadow.

There are other reasons to alert oneself to the shadow's compliments that indicate the shadow of deflation as well. When she was hearing the shadow tell her she was better than Suzy, she realized perhaps that Suzy wasn't at all interested in the decorations either, or that Suzy really wasn't showing off. She might have realized that Suzy was only doing her best and that life is not always black and white, good and bad, and would be reminded of her sense of compassion and equanimity.

She might also have noticed a shadow of inflation towards individuals such as Martha Stewart, who have traits and skills she might envy. She may have identified the reason for her shadow projection—that she needed to take steps to emulate them—and addressed the issue by doing so. She might also have realized that beautiful decorating can take a lot of work, and would have greater compassion for those she wished to emulate, too.

So when your shadow appears, don't feel badly. Realize it's only trying to help you on your way of spirit by showing you how *not* to live. So beautiful is your shadow that you can even accept it for its often troubling ways, and treat it with the care it deserves. You need to simply be alert to its ways, and help it help you get to where you need to be, given its lousy directions.

Don't fear your shadow: fear only what happens when you lack the discernment to see through what it says. In this, you'll want to have a bit of a wider scope and learn what happens when the shadow takes hold in your world.

Key Ideas: How to Manage Your Shadow

- You are inherently good. You project shadow onto the world what you find "bad" or troubling in yourself, such as things you feel are violations.

- To fight shadow with more shadow is not the answer. The shadow can only be managed through love, starting with love for yourself.

- Your contrary self will help you let go of your expectations about how you, and life, should be.

- Trust your essence to help whenever you need it. When you need to, forgive yourself, take a breath, thank yourself for the beautiful things you have, and bask in the glow of your love and the love of the Universe.

- The *IDEA... Identify, Define, and Effortlessly Address your beliefs* practice will help you love yourself in ways you don't yet. (See page 193 for a condensed version of the practice.)

- Addressing to the issues your shadow points out puts you on the path of your life's intent and helps you realize your deepest desires.

- Don't fear your shadow: fear only what happens when you lack the discernment to acknowledge and address what it tells you.

Chapter 13: The Shadow in Your World

When you want things in your world that are not in line with your way of spirit, you get shadow. And when, through your practice, you allow the shadow to help you realize what you truly desire, you allow yourself to ease your fears and doubts. But when you ignore what your shadow tells you, and set out to get only your unnecessary wants met, you will unleash your shadow in ways that would be described as evil.

Compassion for self and others is critical

Evil does exist, but only in your physical reality and not in your way of spirit, for evil can be defined as *compassionless action*. Compassion is your key to ensuring that your shadow projections do not happen and therefore limit the shadow projections in your world.

So take heart: your wanting to express only compassion is the right thing to do. In this, you will—in every way, in every action—express your greatest selves, and will be your happiest self. When you express compassion for yourself and others, your shadow will leave you alone, but when you don't, it will provide only sorrow.

When the shadow becomes greater than your compassion on a global scale, you get world shadow. When your world shadow wreaks havoc, you will find actions that are horrible.

You will need to undertake your best way of spirit to help unravel the shadow of your world and provide guiding assistance in ways you can find comfort in.

The world is not the biggest place—your spirit is—and you can help resolve your world's problems by ensuring your shadows are in check and working to provide *the means for* peace and harmony. Seeking peace and harmony alone will never provide your world with the solutions it needs, which is why you need to take action to provide the means to achieve them.

Do you understand? You cannot solve the world's problems you're creating by yourself, but you can help to bring about the changes the world needs by providing *your* way of spirit. And you will want to change the world. That's right. Because the world needs changing—you know it does—and you'll do well to seek ways to do so.

We will assist by providing you some helpful tips in the event you wish to take up the challenge that your way of spirit will provide you. We will begin with a brief description of how your beautiful, loving world becomes your fearful shadow world. And you'll need to understand this example in a big way because it is your life we're talking about here, not anyone else's.

To change the world, begin with your own life

Now, when we say "you will want to change the world," we mean that you only need to change yourself. But you are the world, and you are other individuals, so the reason you want to change the world is that you know intuitively that *you are them*. So you need to begin where you are: in your own life. And in this, you will find the peace and serenity you need to allow your best self to thrive while enjoying helping others in profoundly beautiful ways.

You have been raised to believe that your needs come second, but you would be incorrect. Your needs come first, as you've learned from Rose already. But your needs include the desire to help others, and when you allow this, you will find your needs met. For you deeply want to assist, but your training has gotten in your way. So throw out your ideas about wanting only to appease yourself: you can't if you won't involve yourself in your world. And when you do, this will be what makes you happy. So do so. Here's how.

The wants you have don't provide certain things that you need in your daily practices. So when you want things, you may find desires as well, but not always. Don't worry about wanting—you can want—but wanting things you don't truly desire blocks your design for yourself, your intent. And your intent is guided by your belonging-to and aligning-with families of intent.[19]

If you are a Borledim (Nurturer), you must in every way nurture yourself before you can nurture others. If you are a poet, you need to provide yourself your own poetry before you can share it in your world. If you are a Milumet (Rememberer) writer of poetry, you can expect that the poetic self will resonate with your remembrance of your innermost self. If you are a Sumari (Artist) writer of poetry, you will create works that will change the world, starting with yourself. Whatever way you choose, you will provide yourself

---

[19] See *Chapter 4: The Families of Intent.*

opportunities to change the world, and there's no reason to believe you won't. But the wanting is not enough—you need to desire it *deeply*. And you need to desire it *first* for yourself.

Success is in your desires, not your wants

Trust that your desires aren't to have the riches and fame that go along with successful works that change your world. You need to instill your own poetry in yourself first, and when you do, you will loosen up your stronghold of expectations about fame and fortune and be on your way of spirit. For changing the world is a humbling thing, not something that will require your grandest homes, or possessions, or self grandeur. There are no reasons to feel you wouldn't get rich, but to set out with this in mind will only impede your progress.

So lose your wants for attention, fame, wealth and security: you may not find them. You *will* find celebrations, abundance, and joy, and not as the ends, but as the means, for you will already have these once you begin to enjoy your way of spirit in your works.

So don't set the bar so high. Just try to achieve what you can, when you can, allow yourself to be the first recipient of your lovely works, then go into your world with the best feeling about your works. This will take yourself out of your picture in healthy ways while attending to the circumstances to ensure your success. Do we make ourselves clear?

Don't worry about success: it will find you, but only in your way of spirit, and not in your wants.

The success that is provided by your desires is the success you'll want. We'll give you an example.

Say you want to provide an excellent way of spirit for yourself that includes providing a way of spirit for others. You could teach your way of spirit in schools, or in your habits by being an example to others. What do you think is the best way to provide your information? *In your habits.* You would provide your way of spirit to yourself primarily, and this is your best self telling you to be in your world in ways that are somewhat selfish and not focused on fixing others. You would also be providing the best way to find peace and harmony in your world, but only when you practice first with yourself. We'll give you another example.

Say you'll want to buy a racehorse. The racehorse seems like a good idea, but just wanting it isn't totally selling you on the idea. So you think to yourself, "I followed your *Way of Spirit* book and found that I want to buy a racehorse. Is this a good way to use my gifts?" Maybe it is and maybe it isn't. The point is, what do *you* think?

If you want to buy a racehorse to prove your worth, that would not be the way of spirit for you. But if you desire owning the racehorse so that you may enjoy the benefits of caring for it with utmost compassion—perhaps as an expression of your belonging-to intent of Healer and your aligning-with intent of Rememberer—why not? You may find that your care for this beautiful creature may make it a winner and set an example for the rest of the racing world to follow. What's wrong with that? Nothing, as long as your reason for buying the racehorse was to enjoy caring for it.

So when you consider your way of spirit, consider that it is what brings you joy, and you will move mountains. For you have the ability to spread your joy in ways that you may find ridiculous, too.

Give your gifts first to yourself, then to others

We'll provide another example. Say you want to provide a clown act for children. How would you do this? You would examine your potential for ensuring that your intent was assured. In other words, why do you want to do this?

In your Borledim (Nurturer) intent, you may want to provide fun for children in order to nurture your inner world and theirs. In your Vold (Reformer) intent, you may want to have the best jokes that will subtly inspire the children to rip apart the status quo. In doing so, you'd find peace and serenity knowing you inspired a generation of children to not listen unquestioningly to authority. What more beautiful way to go about changing the world than to influence very young children in ways that provide their best experiences as well as expressions?

You'd find many reasons to entertain children in this way, but the reasons are important. And so when you energetically engage children in your clown suit, you will be expressing your best self. And you will want to do that in ways that humbly provide your greatest joy. Do you understand? Your desire isn't to change your children, or anyone — it is to change the world — and you do that by ensuring your needs are provided for first. And your intent is the key.

You are capable of changing the world

We will give you one more example to get you on the path of your intent, for it is extremely important. The way of spirit calls you to do the most sublime and ridiculous things you might imagine. Why not start with the sublime? Let's see… because they are the same things?

You've been taught that you need to get on top of the world in every way: you want the biggest bank account, the biggest home, the biggest set of friends. But in seeking these things, you only allow misery because you may never have these things, and even if you did, would that make you happy? We suggest it wouldn't because you wouldn't be allowing your way of spirit. There's no guarantee that you will achieve these things, or that they would ensure your pleasure, and you would waste your life trying to get them while making yourself miserable. Why would you do this? Because that's what you've been taught.

How would this play out in your world? That's right: you get evil in your world. For the thirst for wealth and power is why you need to get a different take on things. You need to let that thinking go, and ensure foremost that your happiness is satisfied, and to do that, you need to do what you *truly* want in your world, not what you may *think* you want. For wanting what you *truly* want—for your desires to be manifest—is the best reason to take on your evildoers, and it will in every way be your success in your world. We'll explain.

Say you want to provide another way to bank. The banking system encourages people to get rich, but why? What possible reason is there to be wealthy except to buy things? That's right, we're not suggesting that being rich is wrong— just overpriced—for when you realize the way of spirit, you'll find you don't need much to be happy. If you want to be happy, you can just be happy and not worry about money. We suggest money is needed to ensure you get your basic needs met, but more than that isn't really important. And why would the way of spirit *not* allow your needs to be met?

You have provided yourself many beliefs about how your money is managed, and your banking system reflects those beliefs. So the rich get richer, the poor get poorer, and the banks get more than their share of monies in the process.

Why not take on your banks in order to distribute your wealth? Because you haven't yet realized you can. You are fearful of big corporations who have lots of high-priced lawyers. So why not take them on in your way of spirit when you know that we'll assist? Because you haven't had a chance to consider that it would be fun. And in fun, we mean in every way *fun*. And for someone like a Reformer individual, it would be excellent fun to take on your banks in ways that would provide joy as well.

The way of spirit is *always* fun. We mean this only the positive sense, for when you are aligned with your intent, you get the heck out of your way, and you live life to the fullest. When you are in your world in ways that are fun for you, as well as satisfying, you'll take on your bullies—individuals who project their shadow in ways that violate—in ways that are compassionate, too.

The world is a very beautiful place. We want to stress
this because when you talk about the shadow, it
sometimes seems that the world is a bad place. It isn't, it
just gets bad when your shadow projections take over.

So you need to watch out for your shadow projections and address them in yourself when they come up.

You also need to watch out for the shadow projections of others, for they also need to be corrected, and sometimes you will need to be the one doing the correcting. Sometimes you will need to stand up for yourself and others. In doing so you, will feal the love of the Universe working through you. And when you do, you will have fun. For your way of spirit will help you in these situations.

Push back on bullies with wisdom and compassion

The way of spirit will provide you the means to, when needed, invoke your Personal God to take on your bullies in your marketplaces, in your banks, in your governments, and in your everyday life when required. Bullies come in many forms and functions, from your daily struggles with those who want to punish others for not doing enough to help around the house, to those whose actions may cause great suffering. For you will find that there are many forms of bully, you only need to peek under the covers.

For example, while there may be reasons to ensure that others help out around the house in ways that are considerate and healthy, perhaps there is someone who uses it as a means to make others feel bad. For example, why would you get stressed out over the lint screen of a dryer needing to be lint-freed? Indeed, you would only get stressed out over this if you feared that the world would be set ablaze by your filthy lint screen, which wouldn't happen because *you* would clean the lint screen, wouldn't you?

So why would you hassle someone about the lint screen unless you were trying to cause pain? There would only be one reason for this: to bully in subtle ways. So don't worry, you may not want to provide your way of spirit to those who bully you with minor details like lint screens, but you may want to take on those who do more bullying. So this takes many forms, and you'll do well to recognize and sometimes push back on your bullies of your lint screen variety as well.

You might, in this case, respond by saying that you will try to do better, that the dirty lint screen will not cause the house to burn down, and that perhaps the lint screen avenger needn't worry so much. This would help to neutralize the situation and help someone cope with life, as when you project shadow, you suggest that you can't cope with life as well as you'd like. That's why doing the work of taking on bullies with compassion is so important: they are suffering because they have a hard time coping with life.

Earlier we discussed a boy of sixteen who desires a new bike, and who in doing so follows his way of spirit, although society wants him to have a car. Why, we asked, would he listen to individuals who tease him about the bike? This example may be the best one for learning how to respond to bullies, as it is the most obvious.

When you allow others to mock you for following your way of spirit, we so want to assist you in your way of spirit, that you can expect us to help you, and we will. For there is no reason to suffer for your way of spirit, nor do you need to suffer by trying to explain. You only want your way of spirit. You're not doing a bit of harm to those who do not follow theirs.

So why not allow yourself to push back on your friends, or even your enemies, for judging you harshly for only doing what makes you happy? We would help you find words such as "Would you mind handing me that wrench? I need to tighten this bolt," for gentle responses are usually the only ones you will require.

You need joy and fearlessness, not approval

When you want the best things for yourself and others, why want anything else that others try to push on you? Because you're afraid they won't like you. And why you would care about this is what you need to address through your belief practice,[20] for you don't need anyone's approval. Do you understand this?

---

[20] See the Identify, Define, and Effortlessly Address your beliefs (IDEA) practice on page 193.

You don't need anyone's approval
in your world.

This takes some getting used to, because you are so very approval-oriented that you would sometimes rather die than risk someone's disapproval, wouldn't you? Indeed, that's a good assessment of why you want to change, for you have been raised to believe that approval is so very important that you'll do anything rather than risk not getting it.

And your approval makers are such important individuals, are they not? No. They are your government officials, your makers of products, your wanting-of-success individuals who are blinded *themselves* to the true nature of finding happiness. And in this, you'll do well to consider yourself lucky that you have the inside scoop: *that you are as happy as you choose to be, and you don't need anyone's approval or definition of what that should look like.* And when you get this, you will provide yourself only joy. And in your joy, you will find your fearlessness. We'll explain.

Joy is your natural state of being, and fear isn't.
You've been raised to fear too much, but your
fears are only your healthy inner responses to
your situation, and can be helpful when you use
them to your advantage.

Your fears are friends who help you identify the need to take action.[21] In this, your joys make your fears rise into your awareness in ways that you can address them.

For example, perhaps you live in a place that has security in the form of bars on your windows. Perhaps you fear that

---

[21] See the Address and Release Your Fears practice on page 194.

the bars don't provide you enough security from your bandits. In this way, your fear would do you a service in suggesting that you consider doing something about it. Your fear will provoke questions in you. "Should I do nothing? Should I put stronger bars on the windows? Should I move to a safer neighborhood?" You'll get a better response to your questions when you don't fear your answers and trust that things will work out, and that's where essence comes in. So when you trust essence to help address your fear, you get the heck out of your way, and that's a good thing.

What's not good is when you make your fears so very important that you let them overwhelm you. Fear isn't a bad thing, it's just misunderstood. You'll find many reasons to fear, but you'll invite more fear if you don't take action. So when you realize your need to move to a safer neighborhood, do so, let your fear help you, then let it go. But don't fear your fear, for fear is what you need to get into a better situation.

Sometimes you allow fear to become fears on top of fears by thinking, for example, "Oh, it's bad all over. There's no reason to move because I'll only find more reasons to fear." In this, you would be stifling your intuition and therefore finding *more* fear because you don't feel you are loved by us spirits, who are providing you the fear communication to *help* you, not to *harm* you.

Do you understand? There's no reason to fear beyond the fear needed to take action, which we provide through your inner communications, because we always have your back. You need only to listen.

Now, back to your desire for a way of spirit that is fearless. When you sense fear, read it, then take action. So you've come across a political party that spews hatred of others. What do you do? You fear they will take over. And you don't want that. You want to stop them.

What do you do? You speak up. You tell them their ways are hateful and they need to stop. Why? Because you are listening to your intuition, and the way of spirit calls you to speak up. Why would you not do this? Because you fear. Will they call you a liar? Perhaps. Why should you care? Are you so wanting of acceptance from them that you'll care?

Indeed, this is something you would need to look at, and your fear would tell you that as well. Why wouldn't you speak up if a Hitler or another type of criminal mind were to take over? Because if you did, you would die. And what would be the harm in this? You only want to live, and that's admirable, but living in your world isn't the final place, and in this, the bullies get you every time, for your fear of dying is getting in your way of spirit.

So trust that *we are not telling you to be sacrificing yourself for any causes any time soon*, but your fear of death in many ways gets in your way even in your most fear-free environments.

Fear overly stifles your contrary self

You know that some individuals have no remorse—on some levels—with killing others. You know they always have the trump card. But you allow the trump card to be played long before necessary, and in this, you fear they might kill you, and they might. But you need to realize that, in essence, they can't kill you, ever, and while this seams simplistic, it's not. For the way of spirit calls on you to be your eternally loving, beautiful self, not caring if others kill you. Do you understand?

We're not saying get up and take a stand in ways that will have others want to harm or kill you, we're saying that you need to lose your fear of death so as to embrace your essence self and find your fearlessness. In identifying with essence, you will find fearlessness in every way, and even your best words, your best posture, and your best ways of sounding off that you could possibly imagine.

So allow your contrary self to shine and we'll take care of the rest. For your contrary self—as we've said—is your best friend and guide to providing you with your imperfectly perfect responses to your world.

And if you are told you are full of baloney, just allow your beautiful contrary self to love you for everything that you are and respond by saying, "Baloney? I *love* baloney!"

We will provide you with a brief summary of what we've covered, then we will provide you with a scenario we want you to consider when you exclude your contrary self and allow shadow to take over.

The world needs your best expressions

Say you would now like to realize your way of spirit in your world. What would you love to do? Indeed, you would first want to consider your intent, both in your belonging-to and aligning-with family of intent. Then you would find ways to do this in your world for a living, or in a voluntary capacity if that is what you desire. You would allow your essence self to assist.

Then—realizing that you will not be mean-spirited in pursuing your wants and desires, now that you have the best in mind for yourself and for the world—when you are provided opportunities to say what you want, say it, for what you will say will be the word of God. Do you understand?

You have the ability to speak up for God in situations that you find unacceptable, for that

is how God speaks: <u>through you</u>.
Your voice is needed in your world!

Then speak up, sing out, dance if you'd like, anything it takes to express the love you feel inside you. Is that clear? You need to express your best self, and to do that you need to be contrary to offer your best expressions of hope, caring, compassion, and bliss—every beautiful thing that is in you.

And when you are confronted by bullies, you need to stand up for what is good, and that includes yourself. In this, we will always support you. In doing so, you will spark a revolution. And that is exactly how you may revolt against the ways of evil in your world—by following your way of spirit. In doing so, you will avoid what isn't needed—tyranny of thought, of expression, of choices. In doing so, you will in every way change your world.

We want to assure you that you will not allow
only your worst critics, you will allow your best,
most reliable critic—your essence—to assure you
that you are doing the right thing. And you will
inspire others in ways they need.

As you speak out in ways you are inspired to do, you will inspire the world to do so, too. For what do you get when you don't speak up? You get the worst of what the world has to offer.

When the contrary self is stifled, the world suffers

We will share your worst nightmare in your history lesson about World War II. When your Nazi regime was first getting started, they were only providing some lectures in halls, and in providing these, they gained momentum. The thing that would have avoided your World War II was only this: contrariness. If the fellows only would have had more people speak out in support of the things that were good, they would have set the course of history in different ways than were realized.

Instead, many didn't speak up because they didn't want to spoil the climate of expression that at the time seemed more powerful than their own. But in not speaking up, they potentiated the path of evil. This is a viable path, but—as in your way of spirit that involves the provision of material goods only—it is a short one. The reason it's short is because there is so much fear involved that the people who are instigating the activities don't allow their best expressions. So you have a climate of fearful pontification that that subjugates your best expressions. And in this, you get the worst of life: the fear that enables only propagation of more fear, and that is why you need to listen to your fears and take action. For when you speak out against providers of fear, you enable their health, too. Do you understand?

You do no person a bit of good when you stifle
your expressions, not even the people who
won't want to hear your words.

So when you are standing up to the bullies, remember it is in your *compassion* that you will be acting, and when you do this, you help all.

For why did Nazi Germany come into being? It came about because there were individuals who feared that the national health wasn't good enough and they realized they could pin their fears on individuals who represented *their own* perceived flaws and lacks. And why? Because they projected their shadow.

So why did they lose the war? Because essence made sure of it. The essence you know would not allow the Nazis to realize world domination. We will not allow such a thing to happen if there is no realization in your process, and there was no valuable outcome that would have been provided if Germany had won your wars. Do you understand? We will prevent things like that from happening when you have no chance of gaining value from it.

So what did you learn in the process? Perhaps nothing if you do not appreciate that the way of spirit required your contrary self to speak up to the bullies to ensure they didn't get further than they did. You could have been spared much suffering.

Essence will help you take the right actions

So when you are thinking about what to say or how to say it, know that we are there to assist and you will find the words. And when you do, you will prevent the shadows of your world from blocking your spirit world. For your Nazi Germany would have been averted and instead been only a few dialogs in your beer halls that would have had spirit invested there, too.

Realize we are providing a very strong example here, and you may find it to be extreme, but it's not. When you lose your sense of freedom of speech that wants to express your contrary self, you might as well be in prison. We suggest you take on your bullies that provide hate speech, hateful actions that cause suffering, and hateful ways of riding the coattails of powerful movements that only to project shadow and pain on others, and do so with compassion.

When you feel threatened, we suggest you do the opposite of the thing you fear would happen. For example, if you fear you will be robbed because the bars on your windows are not strong enough to keep out a bandit, rather than suffering in inaction by believing that the whole world is unsafe, or creating stronger bars because you feel that's the only thing you can do, consider finding a place of safety with no bars on the windows. Expect that we will intervene to increase your power and provide you comfort from suffering. And you know why: *because we are you*. And we want you to be your best self.

So take on your bullies, and—by God—you will create the best world for yourself you could possibly have. And when you feel that you want only to hide, that is when you want to come out of hiding. For that is why you want to hear Rose's words: *you want to no longer hide*.

So take our worst scenario and find ways to apply it to your world. For you have the power to provide your world with better expressions, as well as head off entire armies. Do you understand? That is exactly what you'll do by allowing your expressions. You will win wars. And that is a good thing to do, as winning wars is necessary at times, but preventing them is better.

We trust you will keep reading, dear ones, for we will provide you more reasons to follow your way of spirit... enough to feed an army!

Key Ideas: The Shadow in Your World

- *Evil* can be defined as compassionless action. It is not an absolute Truth, and therefore not as powerful as Love or Compassion.

- Compassion helps ensure your shadow projections do not happen and limits the shadow projections in your world

- Seeking peace and harmony alone will never provide your world with the solutions it needs. You need to take action to provide *the means* to achieve peace and harmony.

- Enjoy your way of spirit first in your works for yourself, then find beautiful ways to help others. You will be guided by your belonging-to and aligning-with families of intent. (See *Chapter 4: The Families of Intent.*)

- Changing the world is a humbling thing. Just try to achieve what you can.

- You will get the success you desire. You may get attention, fame, and wealth, but wanting them will impede your progress.

- The way of spirit provides the means to invoke your Personal God to take on bullies of every variety. Gentle responses and speaking out in support of the good are usually all that's required.

- You are as happy as you make yourself out to be, and don't need anyone's approval. The Identify, Define, and Effortlessly Address your beliefs (IDEA) practice will help you address your limiting beliefs. (See the IDEA practice on page 193.)

- You need to lose your fear of death so as to embrace your eternal, essence self and find fearlessness, even in those situations where your life is not threatened.

- You need to express your best, contrary self. When confronted by bullies, act in compassion, and if you can, stand up to them.

- Essence will prevent catastrophic outcomes when there is no chance of gaining value from them.

Chapter 14: The Way of War

W hen you need a way out of a situation, what do you do? You might allow essence to help make a change, such as taking a break or getting a job you like better. If you could find no options to provide you success, perhaps you would need to change *yourself* instead. But if you didn't realize this, or were unwilling to change, what would you do? You would blame others.

Shadow projection can escalate into war

You can easily see how you could do this on your grandest scale, as even "holy" wars are basically the same thing: they are the outcome of frustration with self that projects shadow onto other individuals in your life—for example, your neighbors.

So when you want to change your situation in ways that are beneficial to you, but you don't have the means or the fearlessness, that's what you create: war. And you'd do well to consider how you create wars in every way, by looking at your own self and what you would accomplish. For there are no victims, only individuals who want things to be different but can't allow themselves to break free of their powerlessness. In this, they want to be freed, and want to free themselves, but cannot, and the frustration that occurs is what causes things to break.

So when you feel that you want to take action, and you cannot find the power in you to change, you need to provide yourself a sense of power for your actions, and this is the point. When you don't, you upend your situation by projecting shadow, then allow your shadow to dominate the situation. But this is futile—as you've seen—and the shadow will not help to remedy your situation. The shadow only escalates into war.

For example, your terrorists want only some respect in your world, but they do not respect themselves enough to allow your world to help them, because the world cannot provide the respect they need from themselves. So when you project war towards them, it doesn't help, it only fuels the flames. And you need to end it, period.

Policing in love is the way to prevent war

There's no reason to believe that fueling the flames of war will in any way help solve the problem of war. Indeed, the fueling is a result of your own shadow projections on the world that you fear. So you create wars through your own actions—your saber rattling, your hatred towards those who you think will cause you harm.

Make no mistake: we are *not* excusing the terrorists from their actions. We are saying that they will not be stopped through hatred or like actions. They will be stopped through the loving compassion and force that is policing in love. And when you do this, you will end the wars. We will explain.

The wars you see on your television sets are projections of
your own fears. We want to repeat that in case you overlooked
the sentence the first time.

*The wars you see on your television sets are
projections of your own fears.*

And when you realize that you have the ability to
immediately turn the dial to another world that is loving, you
will see your terrorists as the truly suffering individuals they
are. We want to assure you that you will be looking at the
same television, but turning the dial is what you do when you
see with your *hearts* what the senseless acts of cruelty in the
world are: they are projections of fear.

When you see the world in this light, you will no longer
want to wage war in your own lives. You will see how every
individual suffers, especially those individuals who seek to
provoke more suffering, as they are only projecting their own
shadows.

So what do you do when you come across a terrorist? You
speak with them. You concern yourself with their welfare.
You assure them you are not their enemy. You assuage your
own fears by resurrecting your wonderful Christ, as he is the
one who said, "Love your enemies as yourself." For you
would understand what he knew: that there are no enemies—
only brothers—and you'd do well to remind yourself of this
teaching.

What you will find in this is your own friendship in Christ,
if that is your religious background. Christians at times want
to follow his words, but not emulate his deeds. And isn't this
the way of spirit? To emulate your Christ's deeds in helping
others to find their own personal heaven? In doing so, do you
see how you must be your best, Godlike self?

Indeed, isn't this the point of the Christian teachings, to ensure compassion in your world and to try to end suffering?

Your Christian, Buddhist, Hindu, Moslem,
and Jewish traditions are exactly the same
when they say "Love thy neighbor."
In this respect, they are all the same.

So what is there to be fighting about? Indeed, only your most violent individuals would find something to use in each tradition to provide the necessary reasons for doing what they want: to hate. So trust that there is no religious reason for any war. You create wars to end them, and you'll do well to end them, but this will not occur by wanting peace and harmony alone. There is not a single thing wrong with peace and harmony, they are just not the only means required to end wars, or to prevent them. We will explain.

Turn the other cheek in forgiveness, not inaction

When your brother does something to you that causes suffering, what do you do? You might impede him by protecting yourself. If you couldn't protect yourself, what would you do? You might ask your parents to intervene on your behalf. And if that didn't work, what would you do? You would need to fight back, wouldn't you? For as much as you want peace, you would rather not suffer while getting it, so you need to *do* something, correct? If you were to simply sit and take the blows, what would that do to help your way of spirit? Nothing.

So it is important to keep in mind that pacifism works in ways that improve some things, but not others. Pacifism has its place when you are in front of a social movement, not behind it. When you help initiate a social movement, you can articulate terms in peaceful ways, such as in acts of nonviolent resistance. If negotiations break down, the means toward peaceful reconciliation become less probable, and the errors in the negotiation process break into schisms that too often lead to violent behaviors by those who feel dissatisfied with the process.

So if your brother were to punch you in the face, the pacifistic approach would be to let him punch you again and again, correct? And this is what the Christian ideal of "turn the other cheek" teaches, correct? *No!*

The Christ teachings didn't intend for you to turn the other cheek and never hit back. They teach you to turn the other cheek in *forgiveness*, but this doesn't mean not taking action to end suffering when violence is waged on yourself or others.

The point is to enjoy *compassion* while you're doing what you need to do. And we mean *enjoy*, for there is not a single thing worse than inflicting pain on another, but if you have compassion, you can alleviate suffering while you stop or prevent fearful people from wreaking havoc on themselves and others.

When the world wants you to intercede on your behalf, or on behalf of another, there is usually very good reason for it. When you are faced with, for example, allowing another to pummel someone to death, you need to step in, correct? That's correct. Why? Because you sense there is a violation taking place, and that your love of peace and harmony would not be enough to stop the violence.

So what do you do? You step in. You hit. You bite. You do whatever it takes to love the perpetrator enough to stop them from doing the extreme action they are. For what more would you want than to stop them from hating? Nothing. You would only bring pain by not allowing yourself to take action: not just *your* pain, and not the just pain of the person being hit, but the pain of the perpetrator as well.

So when you do nothing under the guise of turning the other cheek, you miss the point. The way of spirit calls on you to protect the way of spirit for others.

So do so, and we will assist, always, for that is why you came into the world—to make it better—and every act of generosity and love in every way wants to be heard and seen. We will continue to express that you are the best persons for the job, as you are essence. So do so, and when you do, you will end wars. Here's why.

You can prevent and end wars

When you go to war, it is because your world has escalated the small hurts into big ones. When people get upset about their way of life not being good enough, they hurt, and their hurt grows the more they talk about it, and that hurt turns into whole countries hurting, and then hurt grows to encompass the surrounding areas.

And what would you do to make things better? The same things you would do if your brother were to harm you. You would, for one, begin by protecting your families and your personal property. If your wealth and property are so vast that they require an army to protect them, then there you have it: war.

Do you see how the wars you create are merely the provision of extreme protection of wealth and property? Do you understand that this is what fuels the action of war, including your kingdoms, your feudal states, and your tribal warfare? Indeed, doesn't your wanting protection of your nation's wealth and property aid and abet those who call for warring with other countries that don't have much to do with that?

That is, why would you strike out against a country that didn't have anything to do with what you own? Indeed, there may be reasons, which leads us to our next way of finding peace in your home: putting up your dukes.

> *When you are being bullied, you*
> *need to push back in ways that*
> *potentiate peace.*

When you see someone else being bullied, you need to step in. When you see people suffering in ways that seem to be flourishing, but are not, you need to step in as well.

We'll provide an example. Say you want to go to your cousin's house, and she is a big talker. She loves to talk about all the wonderful things she does and sees, and you want what she has. What do you do? Do you take her things? No, you try to emulate her so you can have your own things. When you have things, you don't want others' things, do you?

So when you want something that someone else has, what do you do? You try to emulate how they got the things, not take them. And when other countries see things that your country has, you want to help them obtain those things, not allow them to take yours. Do you understand the difference?

Your ways are to allow abundance, not extend into realms of suffering by feeling guilty about what you have. There's no reason for this, unless you feel guilty about what you have because you've gotten it in corrupt ways. So if you're guilty about what you have, you may want to consider giving into your way of spirit and giving it away. That's correct, just give it away.

*The extremes you go through to protect what you
have so create your own suffering that you'll do well
without the things in the first place.*

So trust that when a country protects its borders in ways
that might be considered extreme, it's typically not because
they want to protect what they have, it's because they feel
guilty about how they got it, and there would be reason to do
so because they would have gotten it in ill-conceived ways.

So when your border has many guards, you can trust that
your wants have taken over, and you're guilty about what you
have. Trust that you can give away what you don't need, and
get by with less, and you'll have your cousin to thank, because
she taught you that you'll never want for anything as long as
you get what you need, period.

You don't need much, but if your wants have caused the
accumulation of intentionally ill-gotten wealth and property,
then you deserve to lose it, don't you? Indeed you do.

So letting down one's guard is a good thing, and when
you do, you'll get the protection of what you really *need*, not
what you *want*, and let the contrary self discover what's what.
For she will help you lose what needs to be lost, find what
needs to be found, and fearlessly break down boundaries in
ways that you'll find remarkable. For in your way of spirit,
you'll need less boundaries, for there will be nothing, indeed,
to protect.

How to prevent others from causing harm

Now, back to your brother. Let's suppose you are eating a
sandwich and he wants some of it. If you don't need the whole
sandwich, you might give him some. After all, he's your
brother. If he makes fun of your sandwich because it's

something he doesn't like, offer him some anyway. Just say "Here, have a bite." If you need the entire sandwich, you might tell him where to get his own sandwich. You might teach him how to make one if he doesn't know how. If you feel inspired, you might even make a sandwich for him. In any of these scenarios, you would respond in ways that help him get his needs met while ensuring yours are met, too.

We call this "safing on," or to "safe on." You have made a safe place for your brother to be who he is while ensuring your own safety, too. You've found out how to protect yourself by *not* protecting yourself. You've concerned yourself with his welfare. You've assured him you are not his enemy. You've found out that you only need to push back a little and stop being so defensive. He'll back down when he feels safe. But if he doesn't, that's when you take action. You let him know that he'll be "sat on" if he continues.

When you feel that others are taking more than their fair share, then they need to be sat upon.

> *"Sitting on" someone is not the same as punishing someone—it's a way to deter them from causing more harm.*

For example, you sit on others when you provide them with feedback that says their ways are incorrect. You sit on others when you fine them or put them in jail.

In your brother's case, if, after you have acted out of concern for his welfare, he escalates the situation and tries to harm you, you might literally sit on him, and may request the assistance of your parents or other authorities. And when you do, you would give him and any bullies that need sitting on the respect, kindness, and mercy they long for. You would give them your compassion.

Do you realize how many individuals need that to happen?

Do you understand how many brothers and
sisters you have in the world who don't realize
that others care about them enough to provide
them the means to get happier?

That's correct—*get happier*—for their ways do not create happiness, only suffering. So when you sit on them, you get them into the best place you possibly can for their own awareness, to help bring into their consciousness the means to be the best people they can be. And this means judging their *actions*—not *them*—for judging *others* is a futile expression of shadow, and will in every way, in every case, fail you. Judge the behaviors in order to provide individuals the best feedback you can with regard to their way of spirit. For these individuals aren't bad people, typically, they are only wanting your help. So do so.

Now, if your brother objects to your sitting on him, you have one more recourse, and that is to go to the authorities and have them step in, and in some cases, "step on." Stepping on is needed in extreme situations, and this will probably be avoided by sitting on. Stepping on can include forceful actions such as invasion, conviction to prison for long periods, and even death.

Now, the example of your brother wouldn't justify these courses of action, but every home has an individual who needs to be sat upon sometimes, and some who need to be stepped upon, and this happens everywhere. So, for your purposes, consider that terrorists are born in every type of neighborhood, and in every kind of tradition, so your ideas about who they are may need to be upgraded. The terrorists are *you* in many ways, so you'll do well to provide them your most sincere compassion and forgiveness. We'll explain, for this may seem contradictory, but it is not.

You must end suffering where possible

Suffering hurts those who perpetrate it, even though it doesn't always seem like it. When you find someone who doesn't suffer when they perpetrate suffering, you have what is considered a pathology. This sounds like a bad thing, and often it is, but not in every case, for some pathologies allow for health and some do not. We'll give you some examples.

When you are a child, you may pull the wings off of flies or other bugs. You do this with no knowledge that you are doing wrong, you just don't yet know what it means to suffer. But when someone pulls too hard on *your* arm, you realize that what you did to the poor bug was a violation that caused suffering.

When you suffer, you may want to strike out against the perpetrator who caused you to suffer and make them suffer so they can see what it's like. But that would only cause more suffering, not only for you, but for the other individual.

So what do you do? You forgive them. And *that* is what Christ meant when he said turn the other cheek: that you don't cause suffering when you have suffered. Isn't this beautiful? Indeed, if everyone did exactly that, there would be no hardship, only love. But the problem is, not everyone is capable of understanding this because they do not realize how they cause suffering, as they have not learned empathy, meaning that you always have some degree of suffering when you cause the suffering of others.

When you see suffering, you want to end it. Not everyone is like this because they don't know yet what that is. So what do you do to end the suffering of those who do not know what suffering is, and inflict suffering on others without causing their own suffering? You find the most compassionate way to end their suffering, and there are times when killing in ways that end suffering is less a violation than not taking action.

Essence is your best guide in difficult situations

It is *always* a violation to kill, but sometimes the violation is worse when the circumstances provide more suffering if you don't kill the perpetrator. When you have individuals strapped with bombs in your schools threatening to blow up hundreds of schoolchildren, what do you do? You must take them on, for in *not* providing support for the schoolchildren, you are aiding and abetting terrorists. Do you understand?

We are not—truly not—saying that you are correct to kill. We are saying you need to be on your way of spirit to appreciate that killing is sometimes required in order to stop suffering.

And when you do, you will be most fearless, because you will be able to trump the terrorists, finally. You will put aside your ignoble, head-in-the-sand, providing-of-suffering ways of those who wouldn't think twice about killing you or your family and who are themselves suffering. You will realize that life isn't always clear-cut, but is a very contradictory affair for which there are not always perfect, easy answers. Individuals have the ability to terribly wound, kill, or maim, and if they attempt to do that to your peace-loving neighbors, you must take action. And when you do, you will be doing the work in your world that you need to.

When you find that sitting on individuals will not work, that is when you need to step on them *in compassionate ways*, not in uncompassionate or evil ways, do you understand?

Your way of spirit is never to embrace or cause suffering, but to end it where possible.

And in allowing yourself to take the high road, you may need to make difficult decisions that will not have easy outcomes.

Hopefully you will not take this on in your lifetime, but remember—you have many of them—so why not consider that you have the same power as the many terrorists you will encounter in your many probable lifetimes? Why not consider that you have as much or more power as others do? Because you've been afraid of doing the wrong thing. But if you are sitting back in your comfortable chair allowing others to suffer, and you have the ability to end their suffering, then you *are* doing the wrong thing.

You need to know you have a responsibility. And when you feel that you *could* act as we suggested, you'll feel better, because you'll now know that *it probably won't be required.* Do you see what we mean? In the very act of *knowing that you would take action when needed,* you would be fulfilling your destiny in ways that you'll find provocative as well as fearless. So don't be afraid, just trust your inner guides, and when they suggest that you do something to relieve suffering, do it, and we will assist.

When you understand that suffering can be relieved, and that we will help, you will be relieved of your very big burdens. And while you may believe your fears and suffering are inconsolable, we'll console you, and we will also help remove them, which is even better.

Key Ideas: The Way of War

- War is the outcome of escalating frustration with self that projects shadow onto other individuals. There is no religious reason for any war.

- The way to stop bullies and end wars is not through hatred or like actions, but through loving compassion and force—policing in love. In this, judge *actions* not *people*.

- To "turn the other cheek" in forgiveness doesn't mean not taking action to end suffering. It means not making others suffer because you have suffered.

- To stand up to bullies is to respect and care for them enough to deter them from causing harm, including harm to themselves.

- Many wars are caused by the extreme protection of personal property. If you're guilty about what you have or how you got it, consider giving it away.

- When you are being bullied, you need to push back in ways that potentiate peace, not war.

- To take on someone who is bullying you or others, first *safe on* by pushing back gently without being overly defensive. This usually ends bullying. If it continues, you may need to *sit on* to prevent further harm. If needed, ask authorities to intervene. To *step on* is the most serious action, and will hopefully not be required.

- You need to lose your fear of death so as to embrace your essence self and be fearless, but not necessarily to take a stand in ways that others will want to harm or kill you.

- Killing is *always* a violation, but doing so to end suffering is sometimes needed and less of a violation than not taking action.

Chapter 15: Suffering is the Result of Fear

When you see suffering, you have a response that goes to your core. You empathize with individuals in ways that remind you that you are them, and in doing so you remind yourself that you are connected with them in your sense of Godness, or All That Is.

What other reasons would support the idea that when you find suffering, you suffer also? What other possible reason is there? Indeed, suffering has a purpose, and that is to remind you that you are very good, and you are very God. And in this, you will find peace.

There is suffering, but there is also unnecessary suffering that is provided when you fear, and that is most of what suffering is: fear. When you lose your fears, you will find less suffering, and may end it. In spite of what your religions have spoken about, suffering is not a sacred thing. Indeed, there is no need for suffering except to end it. So do so. We will give you some examples.

Fear helps you know to take action

When animals fear, they take action. We've provided an example of how you would address your fears by taking action to protect yourself from intruders by moving to another location.[22] This is what animals do when they move from one cave to another to ensure their safety. Like them, you would, in your way of spirit, welcome the fear so you would know to take action to ensure you were protected. Then you'd find release from your fear, and that is what it is for.

Fear is to allow you to notice a danger to your situation, and when you find ways to take action, you no longer need to fear.

If you had, when fearing your safety, taken no action instead of moving to a safer place, you'd compound your fear with more fear, and rationalize your inaction by suggesting to yourself that "it's bad all over." For when you justify inaction, you compound the problem and create more fear. So when you fear, it is nature's way of saying "take action," and you'd do well to emulate the animals. For once they take action, they don't need to fear until again there's good reason to.

Depression results from fear and inaction

Now, when you sink into depression, you fear what? You fear the future. You fear the past. You fear your life. You fear everything. Why? Because you don't take action. You compound the problem of inaction by creating more inaction, and all you need to do is follow your way of spirit. Do you understand? You're depressed because you're not only *not* allowing your way of spirit, you're moving in ways that are detrimental, layering fear on fear on fear until you end up with a Problem Bermuda Triangle that sinks every hope you have.

---

[22] See the Address and Release your Fears practice on page 194.

The way to beat the suffering
caused by depression is to act.

Taking even the smallest actions when you're depressed will assist in your recovery. For only fear is at work, and it is good to be able to fear when you need to. But when you don't need to fear, you only create fear *on* fear, and fear *of* fear, and that is the bane of your society: you fear too much. You need to take action, be on your way of spirit, and breathe in your new selves that are waiting in your wings to take center stage. For your suffering is just that—fear—and you'll do well to remove it.

Now, what is it about life that requires you to fear so much? Why do you fear the things you enjoy? Because you fear that you will lose them, and you may. But the way of spirit helps you to realize that you never lose them, too. Your wanting only constancy is truly beautiful, but that's not how the world works. You want constancy, you want immortality, but you can't have them in your physical world. But you have them in essence, and in remembering this, you will fear much less. For your provision of essence will be your saving grace in every way, and will impact your fear more than you could possibly imagine. For fear is only the lack of faith, and you can impact your life as well as others' by providing yourself a little faith. Not a lot, just a little goes a long way. We'll explain.

Now, when you get tired or depressed, why do you not rest? Because you fear that life is too short and that you'll miss out on something. Why would you believe this? Because you've been taught that you will die, but you won't, we promise. So why fear that you would miss out on something and therefore not take adequate care of yourself? Because you fear death. And what else goes along with your fear of death? Why, just about everything.

Fear of death creates more fear and suffering

Because you fear death, you make everything about that, and have even perpetuated the belief that death is, in every way possible, a defeat.

Why do you see death as a defeat? Death is death. It's what you do when you die. And there's no reason to believe for a moment that there's anything incorrect about it.

You die in physical terms, but not in nonphysical terms, for your reality is not limited to the physical, is it? You've exposed yourself to the idea that you are immortal, so knowing this, what will you do differently?

Will you believe that the dying need to be continually encouraged to defeat the inevitable? Why would you try to make people suffer in this way? For you to recommend to the dying that they need to fight to stay alive is cruel and unbecoming of individuals who, after so many years of induction into the ways of spirit in religious teachings, would still refuse to believe that this was incorrect, but it is. For you to ignore the fact of death causes much more suffering than you need to have. And in this, you'd do well to commit to living every day like it's your last, for in some ways it is.

Each day you live will not be exactly the same way as the day before. That is the good news and the bad news, for your days will only be better as long as you continue to pursue your way of spirit. And in your way of spirit, you will eventually die: yes *you*. So trust that there is purpose to this, and realize that there are ways to include suffering in ways that are not suffering. We will explain.

You enjoy suffering, do you not? We are joking, of course, and it is a bad joke, perhaps, but you sometimes do enjoy suffering. You may find it very admirable as well as holy, in some respects, but it isn't. Suffering is not one bit holy, and you can find no piece of religious scripture that is worth its salt that says it is. So why do you ensure your suffering is considered holy? So you can do it guilt-free. And to find ways to escape your guilt is the key, not ways to find suffering holy.

Suffering is the content of your fear. When you suffer, you are in fear. When you fear, you don't suffer, you just fear. But when you suffer in fear, you can find ways to not suffer, and that is to connect with essence. For essence always wants to provide condolence as well as end your suffering.

Trust essence to relieve your suffering

When animals suffer, they don't fear it, they just go into a state that would be considered out-of-body. They do this for self-preservation, for their fear wouldn't assist: that's not what fear is for. Remember, fear helps you know to take action. So when you suffer, and are past taking action, you need to remove the pain. And the way to do this is to surrender to essence, for you suffer when you insist that only your actions will make it stop. For what is fear but suspension of the belief in essence? Indeed, in connecting with essence, you will fear less and therefore suffer less.

We'll give you an example. As we said, when your animals suffer, they find ways to end suffering by turning themselves over to essence. When they feel sick, or are curtailed in their ways of greener pastures, they find ways to allow themselves relief in essence.

Do not make the mistake of believing that you are off the hook in providing better lives for animals, you are not. But you can take some comfort in your realization that essence is in every way in charge, and we would not allow punishment. But you are aware that there are circumstances where animals are treated cruelly, and this is for your purposes: to find relief for them.

In doing so, make yourself helpful by ensuring that animals are your happiest companions in spirit. For spirit is imbued in animals in ways that are truly, spiritually significant, and your treatment of animals reflects how you want to be treated by essence. In doing so, learn to incorporate what animals know, for they can teach you much.

Animals are your greatest teachers

Animals are the best friends you have in spirit, for they will tell you their wonderful secrets: the secrets of the Universe.

Animals know they do not die, they know they are immortal, they know they need not live in perpetual fear, they know to listen to their fears to take action, and they also know that they can rely on essence always. Isn't that exactly what you need to learn?

So take lessons from the animals, as the way of spirit is imbued in them in ways that are quite natural. And when you feel that you are superior to them, consider that you are also inferior to them. Do you understand? Just because you have evolved in ways that provide you a glut of riches does not in any way provide you permission to feel that you are better than animals. When you realize this, you will truly address the problems of the world. We'll provide examples that will make you laugh.

Have you ever seen an orangutan belch loudly? They do it, and they do it well. The reason they do it well is that they have no fear that someone will judge them on how they look or smell or dress funny. They have no compunction in any way, only a natural grace that is spiritual. And they laugh in ways that are funny, because they allow their laughter to ring out into the world.

And in this—you're saying to yourself—why would you want to be like the orangutan? Because you *are* the orangutan. You *are* the cow. You *are* the kitty cat. You *are* all the things in your world. And when you surprise yourself by allowing your best, most wonderful expressions, you allow your animal self to see you through your troublesome times. That's right, for your animal self—the self that you have evolved from—is always in you and always will be. So when you fear fear itself, you can call on your inner animal to help you.

You've been brainwashed—yes *brainwashed*—to believe that man is superior to all of life that you create the best reasons for extinction, for your superior attitude has resulted in the disappearance of your forests, your jungles, your apes, your elephants and hundreds of other species. And why? Because you don't appreciate them. And why is that? Because you don't allow yourself to embrace life. Your presupposed beliefs that were to prepare you for being in the world have left you ill-prepared for life. You need to ensure you are taught better before going into the world. To do that, you need to embrace your inner animal.

The definition of animal that we'll use is *a subordinate species to man*. The way you sometimes think of yourselves is as animals grown up and ensure that the animal parts of you are quite dead. But this would be wrong—as well as foolhardy—for in your interpretation of subordinate, you forget that the *ordinate systems are totally reliant on the subordinate ones.*

Do you understand? The subordinate species that you look down upon are the very ones you rely on for survival. And when you frown on them, thinking how inferior they are, you frown on yourself. And you deny yourself the many gifts that they provide you besides the meat, and fur, and eggs, and cheese, and myriad other products. You're only seeing half of the picture when you only see the exteriors. The interiors are also important, and possibly more so.

Animals don't fear the way you do, as we've said. They don't respond to threats the way you do either, for they have no need to punish. They will allow sitting on others when they aren't doing things they want, but they will not punish. They will indeed kill, but this is to survive—not to punish, and not to take out the bad guys, because in their world, there are none.

Their species are so remarkable that they have no pathologies, only health, except in some extreme cases, such as those who have been caged in ways that cause them suffering. In this, there are some cases of suffering, but this is assuaged by essence, and in many cases, essence will intervene and cause the death of the animal in order to relieve suffering. This is often the case of rats in laboratories, and there is reasonable evidence that the simple act of caging them causes death. So when you consider your test results, keep in mind that they are very skewed. And that is only one example. There are many ways in which essence assists by ensuring that suffering ceases, which is where we were at the beginning of this chapter.

You'd do well to incorporate the fearlessness of animals in all ways, at all times, for essence works in animals in miraculous ways. We trust you will pay closer attention to your animal friends, so you'll do well to take notes, too!

Now, by the time you read this, you should know all about how animals are your superiors in some ways, particularly in their ability to address and release their fears.

So how do you rid yourself of *your* fears? We suggest that when you follow your way of spirit, your fears will subside, and you won't require sedatives or anti-anxiety medication either, for why would you need this in your way of spirit? Indeed you will not. Take two orangutans instead.

Now, we will summarize what we've taught in the previous chapters.

In a nutshell, you need to fear less and turn yourself over to essence. When you do fear, take the lessons of the animals and be the natural individuals you were designed to be. Then make sure you treat them well. Then make sure you treat yourself well, and others. When others are causing suffering, sit on them. If they fail to respond in ways that will allow their greater joy and health, set aside your concerns about being nice people and step on them with compassion, and you will provide yourself with the loving kindness that is needed in the world as well. For you want to assist, and without the compassionate means of ending suffering, you will provide yourself the same lack of action that continues to plague your species.

So take action, and do so with compassion.

Key Ideas: Suffering is the Result of Fear

- When you see suffering, it reminds you of your Godness. In this way, suffering is purposeful. Otherwise, there is no need for suffering except to end it.

- Suffering is sometimes considered holy so that one may live guilt-free. The way to escape guilt is to address the beliefs that cause it. (See the Identify, Define, and Effortlessly Address your beliefs (IDEA) practice on page 193.)

- Most suffering is unnecessary, the result of fears that have not been addressed and released. (See the Address and Release Your Fears practice on page 194.)

- Fear helps to alert you of a situation. When you address it by taking action, you no longer need to fear. When you justify inaction, you create more fear and suffering.

- The way to end suffering caused by depression is to act. Even the smallest actions will assist in your recovery.

- Suffering that is past the point of taking action can be eased by trusting in essence.

- Embracing your immortal essence self and letting go of your fear of death will help release many of your related fears.

- Animals are a subordinate species, not an inferior one. Humans need animals for their survival, in both exterior and interior ways, as models for behavior.

- Your animal self—the self you have evolved from—is always in you and can help you live your best, most fearless and expressive self.

Chapter 16: The Way of Spirit is Yours Now!

The way of spirit is yours now, as well as in your past and future. In other words, you've always been on your way of spirit, but sometimes you just don't realize this. So when you are feeling bad, we will be there in spirit to assist you, as we always have, whether or not you realized it. In this, you've always been on your path, but you just never noticed.

When you speak to God, you speak to essence. When you dream, you speak with essence. When you act with compassion, you do so with essence. When you are sick and miraculously healed, you are healed by essence. Why, only when you are deathly ill or seeking comfort, do you call on us? Because that's when you need us: when you're truly desperate.

We are always here to support you, not to tell you what to do. That's *your* job. We want only the best things for you, and that means butting out of your affairs, but when you choose things that would be harmful to you or the world, that is when we intercede. And you'll do well to notice, for your fear is so very great that you forget who is always in charge: *essence*.

This may sound as if we are contradicting ourselves, but we are not. Why you would choose to have a beautiful set of gods wanting to help you is the very important distinction: so you can try things without harm coming to you. And when you choose to respond with love for self and others to the world—that you, as well as essence, create—you get the way of spirit.

It is *your* way, not essence's. We just help. Essence is you, and your ego would love to believe that it is making all the choices, but when it realizes it has great helpers, it will find more joy and less fear, which is why you have chosen to read this little book.

The way of spirit is *your* way, and yours alone. When you want help, you only need to ask. When you pray, we listen, but we don't always give you what you want because if it's not what you've set out to discover in your desires, you won't get what you ask for. We suggest you feel lucky you don't get everything you ask for, as it would be a big problem, as you ask for things that would take too much energy on your part to achieve and then don't fulfill you.

So when you ask for something like a big car, you may find that you don't want this even after you get it. Trust that we always have your best interests in mind and realize that it's not a good idea to get everything you ask for. But you *can* provide yourself with your desires, and these are the keys to your happiness. When you have your desires met, you are happiest.

> *When you have your desires met, you*
> *give in ways that are beneficial to the*
> *world and are most firmly on your*
> *way of spirit.*

But don't worry: you'll always be on your way of spirit, for your wanting things provides you the means to let go of things you need to. In this, you will create wars, obstacles such as illnesses, and strike out at the world in ways that do not support your growth. And you will notice that this doesn't make you happy one bit. You'll see that there are many different approaches to living life, and your happiest way is your way of spirit—not anyone else's—*yours.*

When you discover this path, you will have a most beautiful journey, and you will provide the best self you can be to yourself and to the world. And that's important to understand, because if you are not living your best life, you can't be useful to others.

Soothing your own hurts and problems is the first order of business, then you can think about how to be in your world helping others.

There's a big difference between using your gifts to assist the world when you're personally comforted than it is to be in your world with no way of comforting self. Your products will be completely different. That's why you must first focus on self, and we will assist. We'll explain.

We've given you a great many words to describe our way of spirit to you, but know that we want to commend you also on your choice of finding Rose. For we are here to assist on your way of spirit, which as we've said, you've always been on. To understand how this is true, provide yourself a big dose of forgiveness, for your need to forgive yourself for any past indiscretions is necessary for your continued happiness.

When you get on your case too much, you need to engage your essences to help you see the reasons why you went through what you did.

You don't need perfection, and while you do need to take responsibility for your transgressions towards yourself and others, you don't need to beat yourself up over any of the things you did out of pain or ignorance.

We want you to give yourself a big dose of forgiveness so you can embrace your wonderful path, and also to forgive the many individuals who have hurt you. They are essence, too. They wanted only the best things for you.

Your hesitancy to find your desires and live your bliss is why the things in your past happened, isn't this correct? It was never about the way you *did* do something, it was always about the way you *didn't* do something, and in *doing* something you will learn what your heart's contentment is all about. In this, you have learned well, for the individuals in your life have taught you to be in your world with all of the desires you can muster.

> *It was never about what you lacked, it*
> *was always about what you had but*
> *were too afraid to show. So don't let*
> *your own insecurities get in your way.*
> *You were fearless once.*
> *You can be fearless again.*

And what makes a fearless individual? It is your lack of fear of harm, and we've explained how that is very real. No one can harm you. You only harm yourself when you choose to stifle your best selves. So don't.

> *Take life into your hands and cherish it*
> *like you were born to do, then live it.*

Now we will provide a summary of things you may do to assist yourself. These are not hard-and-fast rules, only a few suggestions to get you on your way.[23]

First, find your intent. This is your essence's design for fulfillment, and what we would call your destiny, not in the sense of a single path that you must take, but in many probable paths essence staked out for you. Provide yourself with your belonging-to and aligning-with families of intent to help you discover the path your deepest expression. For the path is there, but you may not yet see it, and the families of intent are designed to assist, not edict. Use them well, for you will see that they are extremely potent tools that will become familiar to many. Don't get too hung up on your own families and create tribes. Remember, they are designs that essence employs to create your physical reality: you are comprised of *all* of the families, all at once. So use them wisely.

Second, define your intent name. Your intent name expresses why you decided to become physical. It could be Protector of Children or Healer of Homes or Beautiful Dancer. The best names will more or less align with your families of intent, so choose well. These will help you achieve what you want to achieve, as they proclaim your intent in the world, and are desperately needed. So do so.

Third, realize your essence name. Your essence self has a name—an essence name—which you can discover by asking your essence to tell you through your deep intuition. The name may be unlike any you've ever heard. And though essence is neutral in gender, the name and fealing tone may

---

[23] See the Intent Practices on page 189.

be masculine or feminine. The important thing is that the name resonates with you most deeply.

Next, learn how to channel your essence. You have the ability to speak in ways that would be considered divine. To do so, focus on your intent, then find ways to bring your inner world into your outer world in ways that are least distorted. The Vespers practice will help.[24] You have in you a rich inner world that needs expression, you only need to assure yourself that you can, and then do it.

Next, take the high road in your world. When you are able, take your voice into your world and speak for God. This will occur naturally in ways that you'll find both funny and perhaps a little scary. For when you speak for God, you will surprise even yourself. And don't think you won't, for you will encourage many others to speak out on many fronts, in many ways, too. So do so, and fear not, as you have us essences to back you up. When you suggest to yourself that the world needs improvement, you are correct. So improve it, and do what you can to make the world a better place for yourself and for everyone.

Next, provide assistance to the downtrodden. The world needs you to provide your best selves one day at a time, not to provide assistance only when you are asked. Help others. Try not to disparage those who are in pain due to their own ignorance. You need to be merciful. You are Gods, are you not? So act the way you are, and be in your world in ways that are truly spectacular, not only in your sense of your lifetime, but in your sense of All That Is.

---

[24] See the Vespers practice on page 195.

The way of spirit incorporates for you only magic, and in this, you will see the magical events that happen in and around you in every moment. The way of spirit is an incredible experience in which you will discover that your senses operate most fully, your breath incorporates more air as well as spirit, and your dogged pursuits of happiness melt away without your missing them. For the way of spirit offers more: it offers your most beautiful and spontaneous world in which anything can happen in any moment. Free yourself to live this life that you've always longed for: the life you desire.

The way you will know you are on the right path is if you are happy. Trust yourself to know what your path is. Trust your inner authority—your essence—to determine what is right and what is wrong. Your sense of discernment is an important and powerful superhero ability.

Now you have the final tool in your superhero toolbelt, and are ready go into your world and do great deeds, for you have the power, you have the will, you have the mighty forces of the Divine working through you, and you are the hero of your life. So act in your best interests and in the interests of others—*in that order*—and you will indeed be the savior of your world.

For *You* are the way of spirit—not your ego self, essence self, contrary self, animal self, shadow self, nor the world around you, people in your dreams or probable realities, nor the saints or slummers, angels, ogres, or bogeymen, nor All That Is—but *all these at once*. And when you realize that, you will be your best savior.

For it's not the world that needs saving—it's <u>you</u>—
and to do so, you need to be in your world.

We trust you will!

Practices

Practices are small, regular actions that help you live a happier life. They may be things you already do, but wish to do in a different way. When they become habits, they will transform your life.

Access Alternatives

This practice helps you break out of closed patterns of thinking to allow contrary ways to consider something, rather than just the "right" or "perfect" way. You can do this any way you'd like—with or without a poker table, quickly or in a longer meditation. It will help you with almost anything, from making big decisions to relaxing and being in the now.

Imagine a room set up for a late night poker game. There is a table in the center with poker chips, drinks, and whatever munchies you'd like.

Now, allow the alternatives you're considering to drift in as players assembling at the table. There will be one dominant player, a loud and sassy one who postures quite a bit and wears a funny hat. This player is the most obvious alternative that you are starting with. He is going to ante up many chips. And he is the one you want to take to the bank.

The other players will ante up, too, and provide alternatives that you have not considered. They are your contradictory thoughts, saying, "That's not the winning hand, *mine* is!" They might say, "Trust us! We represent a beautiful set of probabilities that you may enjoy much more than his. For god's sake, why would you consider trusting a guy wearing a hat like *that*?!"

There are potentially infinite numbers of hands—or probabilities—worth considering, and some of them will certainly beat the funny hat player's hand. Each player bets that you will be happier with their alternative. *They will also come up with alternatives that you are not yet aware of.*

Now, as you allow your players to inform you of more alternatives, you will notice that one of them has a winning hand. It is perhaps the most wonderful thing you might ever consider, but because you were so distracted by the loud, sassy player attached to the bottom of the hat, you were unable to even see it before.

It doesn't matter which player wins because you are only considering probabilities. You are always the winner. You will always take home all the chips, munchies and beers, and free yourself of the need to invest in any one player or another. You are the chips. You are the players. You are all of the probabilities. So it is incumbent upon you to allow anything to happen because you will be the one who experiences it, and you must not consider one set of potentials too strongly because it prevents you from being in the now.

After you have cleared the table, rest in your awareness without giving too much energy to one particular future outcome or another. With practice, you will be able to do this without the need for the poker table, but this is entirely up to you. We expect you to, in any case, be the winner of every game!

Intent Practices

These practices help you identify and express the superhero qualities that you were born with. For more information, see Chapter 4: The Families of Intent.

Discover Your Family of Intent *Belonging-to*

The family of intent you *belong to* is the one that your essence holds in *every* lifetime. The way you identify the correct family is to trust your deep intuition to tell you, "What way of spirit do I follow at the soul level?"

This may come easily to you, because it is the way of spirit that is in you so deeply that you may take it for granted. Also, it is possible to have a combination of family intents, but for now, you can focus on one or two families.

Then ask your inner self, "What is my best expression—my easiest way of doing things?" In this, your belonging-to family will become clear to you, as it expresses itself naturally and easily for you in every lifetime. You'll find a comfort level with the family of intent that you choose, as you'll be very familiar with it in inner ways. In this, your family of intent belonging-to is considered your *ease area*.

Discover Your Family of Intent *Aligning-with*

Now, the way to find which family of intent you *align with* is to choose the one or two that most attract you and yet sometimes cause you trouble. For example, if you have a Borledim (Nurturer) alignment, you may find it easy to nurture others, but have trouble nurturing yourself.

This is what the alignments are about—*challenge areas* that allow you to investigate other families' unique expressions and help you develop your abilities to their fullest. In this, you'll find a natural aptitude, but it will often have challenges built in. It's as if you get invited to a wonderful party, but there are obstacles along the way and you have trouble getting there.

As with the belonging-to, it is possible to have a combination of aligning-with intents, but for now you can focus on one or two families.

Discover Your Intent Name

Every individual who has ever lived is born with a special intent in life. The intent name is a summation of your intent that will help you understand and deeply resonate with your own special intent and gifts. When you discover your intent name, you will find many things happening in your lives to help you on your way of spirit, for intent names are very powerful things.

To do so, just tune into your greater self to find your natural direction and assign the best intent name that you can, such as Creator of Beautiful Things. You can refine it over time as your path becomes clearer.

Discover Your Essence Name

While your essence is nameless, you can give it a name to help you more deeply identify with and tune into your vast, multidimensional nature, your very own Youniverse.

You may discover your essence name by asking your essence to reveal this name to you, and then be open to receiving it in your intuition and dreams. You may hear it, see it, or just have an awareness of it. The name may be a common one, or be unique, with an unusual spelling and pronunciation. There's no need to rush this: you will know your essence name in time, just trust your intuition.

Sonter (Breathe in Essence)

While breathing would seem to not require instruction, your ego self needs to understand that breathing is not an intrusion into the body to keep it alive: it is a reminder that you are essence.

The best way to change your old habits is to breathe. We mean <u>BREATHE</u>. Breathing was intended to remind you in every moment of your days, in every moment of your lives, sometimes beyond your lives, that we essences are in your selves in every way. You may imagine breathing to be a reminder that although you are physical, you are intimately connected with your invisible world.

There is no separation from essence, ever. The separation was created in order to allow you to explore your physical reality. The way you often think of your physical reality is in materialistic ways, but this is an illusion.

Consider that you are comprised of cells that are materially empty. The atoms that make up your buildings and even your simple constructions are empty in terms of physicality. But there is no emptiness, only consciousness. When you breathe in essence, you fully impress upon every cell in your bodies, in every single millisecond of your days, that you are a divine creation made up of "empty" essence, sontering your way through your Universe.

When you sense your breath as a form of consciousness and not an intrusion, you may relax into your breathing as a beautiful reminder that you are essence, you breathe essence, and all of your creation is exactly as your essence co-creates it with you. We suggest you continue to breathe in your essence in a beautiful and joyous manner, for you are very important and loving individuals who are intimately part of your world in ways you can only imagine! And when you do, realize we essences breathe you, too, as do the many beautiful potentials who call you to them in loving ways.

So breathe, beautiful creatures, <u>BREATHE</u>!

Rest in Rose

To meditate is to relax into a state in which you deeply experience the fealing tone of essence. The experience may be subtle or profound, and will involve emotion only when you are starting out and need assurance that essence is with you. There's no way to do this incorrectly. This practice builds on your familiarity with the fealing tone of Rose—which you have experienced by reading this book—to help you connect with your own essence.

Take a few deep breaths—sonter—and rest in the beautiful, loving sunshine of essence. When thoughts enter your mind, let them pass like clouds in the sky and return your focus to your breath.

Now, imagine yourself enfolded in Rose's loving arms. You might sense yourself resting in the petals of the softest, deepest, and most beautifully scented rose you can imagine. Rose's fealing tone, and your own essence's fealing tone, will be divinely, deliciously senxual. Enjoy this fealing for as long as you'd like.

Next, ask your essence self to speak with you through his or her fealing tone. Your essence may present thoughts, words or images to help you move into that developing space. With practice, the space will become clear and you will be able to move directly into it.

Maintain the state for as long as you can. Engaging essence in this way is very beneficial to your body, mind and spirit.

We suggest doing this practice whenever you can, for whatever length of time is available to you. To return to the meditative state throughout your day, just take a few moments to breathe and remind yourself that we are always here for you. Come back to this place whenever you feal the need to speak to us, or to realize rest and loving kindness.

Identify, Define, and Effortlessly Address your beliefs (IDEA)

This practice builds on the Access Alternatives practice to identify and address your shadow.

When you feel bad for any reason, notice it and *identify* the belief you have that is blocking your nature to be happy, such as fear or doubt you may have. You will need to access alternatives, as the issue will be something you have in the past identified as someone else's problem, when it is really yours.

Then *define* how to address the problem. You may need to let go of expectations about things needing to be certain ways in order to be happy, get your wants aligned with your truest desires, learn how to assist others in ways that gain your satisfaction as well, and myriad things you can do to change the way you think about the issue. Consider the simplest things, and realize that everything in the world has pluses and minuses.

Then *effortlessly address* the beliefs by taking action. You may want to help yourself enjoy your body more by taking a dance class, or take a trip that you've been wanting to do but didn't feel you deserved. You might take action to repair a problem in a relationship that you've not acknowledged before was the result of *your* flaws, not someone else's. The idea isn't to remove beliefs, but to allow them to help you realize how to make changes in your thoughts and actions that will help you get happy.

Address and Release Your Fears
This practice builds on the Access Alternatives practice. For more information on addressing your fears, see page 77.

When you encounter a fear, imagine it is a friend who is trying to help you by bringing an issue into your awareness. If you are going over and over the same thoughts, there is an underlying fear that you need to address.

If the fear indicates something that *is not* in your control, it is because of your ego's insecurity that it is not getting what it wants. In this case, remind yourself that your *essence* self, not your *ego* self, is ultimately in charge and ask essence for help. If the fear indicates something that *is* in your control, take the actions you need to address it. Then thank your fears for their help, and let them go on their way.

For example, say you fear that an event the following day may not go well. Is there something in your control that you can do? Might you prepare for it in a way you hadn't considered before? If *so*, do so. If *not*, you might ask essence to help make the day go well, or to help you enjoy the day no matter what.

Another example: you may fear that global warming will doom the planet and its inhabitants. Since this is *not* completely in your control, you can request that essence assist, then "let go, let God". You may also identify things that *are* in your control. Taking action to do these things—such as living in ways that are harmonious with the earth's ecosystem—will give you peace of mind that you are doing what you can.

Vespers
This practice builds on the Sonter, Rest in Rose, and Access Alternatives practices to help you channel your essence. For more information about Vespers, see page 97.

Vespers are an hour or more of meditation in which to speak with your Personal God. The morning is the best time to do this, as it allows the most penetration from your dreamspace. *Your essence so wants you to do this it will seize you by the pajamas to tell you what you need to know, and that's why we want to stress this so dearly to you.*

First, establish a daily routine that allows you a quiet space in which to rest in the feeling tone of your essence. Ask your essence to speak with you about whatever you feal is important—your dreams, challenges, fears, desires— anything that is coming up for you. Or you may simply ask three questions: What do I want to do today? What do I want to do tomorrow? What do I want to do for the rest of my life?

Next, move into a sense of creative flow. You might sit quietly and let the dreams from the previous night enter your awareness. You might begin a daily practice of opening a blank page and writing whatever comes into your consciousness, then turn your attention to those things. Starting with a blank page will provide you many improbable expressions, some that you may already be investigating, only on a different order, such as alternate forms of banking, of baking, of children's education, of the many interests that you already have. You may wish to write, paint, sing, dance, or anything that expresses what comes through. You might explore ideas and activities that are familiar and probable, and as you continue, become new and improbable.

As you continue your practice, allow yourself to discover and experiment with forms of expression that you feel passionate about. Your passions are things you loved as a child that you may not remember doing, but linger in your intuition like long-ago dreams.

Allow yourself to explore any interest you can imagine. As you continue, the interests you begin with will honor the ones you've almost forgotten, and you'll see that your path has been productive and blissful all along. In this way, your Vespers will turn into what you truly want to do with your life and a means to appreciate how you got there.

Evening Prayers
Prayer is a means to engage your best reasoning and intuition to meditate into the space of non-reasoning. There is no better time to do so than falling asleep to instill a sense of connectedness with your essence. Prayers done before sleep help you collapse the day's events, calm your mind, and lull you into the dreamspace where you will obtain specific help from essence. When you wake, you will find new abilities to know and express your desires (see the Vespers practice). You may wish to prepare by placing a notebook or tape recorder next to your bed to record your dreams. For more information about prayer and how it affects dreams, see page 107. This practice builds on the Rest in Rose, Access Alternatives, and Address and Release Your Fears practices.

To begin, sonter essence and begin an inner conversation. Trust that your essence wants you to have what you desire. Remember that you are talking to a friend who knows you intimately and knows your innate goodness. Ask for what you want or need—this is called *petitionary prayer*—but don't stop there. *Keep going.*

As you relax and open up to essence, let yourself access alternative views. Your contrary self will help you notice new thoughts and ideas coming into your consciousness and give you a sense of what is and is not in your ego's control. For what *is* in your ego's control, you can access ways to address. For what is *not* in your ego's control, you can ask essence for help.

For example, perhaps you fear you will be judged negatively by a group of people, and you pray that you won't be. Your contrary self will help loosen your expectations by suggesting, for example, that even if you throw up on someone, you will still be lovable. Then you find a sense of safety. You realize that people's judgments are not in your control. You discover that what *is* in your control is that you not judge *yourself* negatively. You ask for essence's help in doing that. Then you breathe into the dreamspace while allowing the love of essence to reinforce those feelings of self-acceptance. In the dreamspace, you realize a passion for being with others that you hadn't known before. When you wake, you recall a dream that illustrates this, and move into your Vespers practice with a heart full of love and wonderful new ideas for expression.

You might pray for essence to provide certain, happier outcomes in the world, but you sometimes need to get through the sorting part of petitionary prayer to understand that there are reasons for the world being the way it is at times. You can be happy in the world of sorrows without needing feal that you have to control it: you don't. You sometimes need to accept this, and discover what it is about the situation that *can* control and what you *can* do to remedy it, in ways small or large.

When you allow yourself to not fear the problems that your ego can't solve on your own, you will have more sense of your essence self than you did before. You will realize how everything is as it should be, and move into a sense of equanimity—the composure you feal from holding little judgment and allowing your ego self to relax into a supporting role.

As you continue to pray, you will find your wants distilled into a state of realization that is called *contemplative prayer*, that you may also consider Resting in Rose, or Samadhi, or whatever you want to call it: it is the experience of your essence selves. And when you do, you will count your blessings, and this is the best prayer you could provide yourself. For to determine that you already have exactly what you need, and express your gratitude for it, is the best prayer there is.

Glossary

Access Alternatives – a core practice to help break out of closed patterns of thinking to allow more potentials you may take for any situation, rather than just what is considered the "right" or "perfect" way. This helps you live in the now and become aware of probabilities that may better fulfill your desires.

All That Is – the level of being that is the Totality of All Things and All Probabilities.

channel – to accurately translate inner experience to outer experience through artistry, healing, or other natural, inspired acts in alignment with your intent.

Consciousness – Spirit, Divinity, All That Is.

contrary self – the self who loves you exactly as you are, no matter what. The contrary self helps provide what you need and desire—but not always what your ego wants—by letting you know when you need to question your actions. The contrary self is always loving, and never degrades others or acts in ways that lack compassion.

desires – natural impulses that come from your essence that are aligned with your intent and hold your greatest fulfillment. They are wants that are the healthiest expressions of your selfhood.

Dreamwalker – an essence comprised of many essences who is directly involved with the creation and maintenance of physical reality. Rose describes herself as a Dreamwalker.

ego self – the level of being that is your everyday God-in-training, and often makes choices based on fears rather than the guidance of essence.

energy exchange – the means by which all things—atoms, molecules, bodies, and solar systems—are intimately connected and supported by All That Is. Also defined as channeling an essence other than one's own.

energy personality essence – a vast, multidimensional being who exists outside our physical space-time construction. Rose is an energy personality essence, as is Seth and many other nonphysical teachers who assist in our shift in consciousness.

essence, essence self – the vast energy that you can consider soul, spirit, inner self, greater self, or Personal God—the "spiritual suggestion box" who helps guide you. Your essence has many focuses of attention in many dimensions and timeframes simultaneously, and is always there to assist.

equanimity – the composure you gain from holding little judgment and relying on essence—which includes your ego self—to make the calls, invoking a sense that everything is as it should be.

evil – compassionless action. It is not an absolute Truth, and therefore not as powerful as Love or Compassion.

families of intent – nine characteristics of consciousness that work together to create an infinite number of expressions, including our physical universe. They are guidelines to help find your innate intent and follow your way of spirit.

family of intent belonging-to – your essence's innate intent that is expressed in every focus of attention (lifetime). It is a theme that expresses itself naturally and easily in all of your lifetimes.

family of intent aligning-with – your innate intent that is expressed in this focus of attention (lifetime). It is a theme that is designed to be a challenge area to allow you to investigate other families' expressions.

feal – a combination of *feel* and *real*; the ability to use one's inner senses in the deepest, most accurate, efficient and satisfying means possible. Fealing allows the greatest connection with essence and expression while reducing *theatrics*, which express inner feelings inaccurately, block energy, and take more effort than needed.

fealing tone – a means to identify and interpret specific energy.

flaws – perceived wrongs about self and others that are not wrongs, only things that have not been addressed—such as fears, anxieties, and ways you don't love yourself yet—based upon the incorrect beliefs you've been raised with. You are not flawed from birth, you were born in a state of Grace and will never leave it.

focus of attention – a lifetime such as your own. Your essence self has a vast number of focuses in many other dimensions and time frameworks that exist simultaneously.

geanius – a combination of *gene* and *genius*, your innate spiritual wisdom and genetic codes inherent in your body, which are essence, too, and provide introspective, inspired information. Your way of spirit includes your mind, body, and your very genes. All are intimately connected with essence.

inner moral cooperative sense – awareness of the potential for violation so as to make beneficial non-violating decisions in your now. By choosing to not violate, you live in greater cooperation with All That Is.

intent – your essence's design for fulfillment. Discovering your life's innate intent is an important part of your way of spirit (see families of intent).

God – levels of being that you may identify and explore relationships with; while it's sometimes necessary to describe levels of being, there are no closed systems or divisions in consciousness.

- The everyday God-in-training—the you who makes choices based on your way of spirit (your ego self)
- The mediating Personal God—the "spiritual suggestion box" who helps guide you (your essence self)
- All That Is

love – the moral authority that permits individuals a means to invoke the word, actions, and intent of their essence in the service of self and others.

karma – an action propelled by the imprint of a violation to compel you to learn from your mistake. When you violate another, you also violate yourself.

meditation – to relax into yourself, close your eyes, breathe in your essence (sonter), and experience the fealing tone of essence.[25]

natural time – the inner sense that guides planetary and physical rhythms that include body cycles, tides, sun movement, and seasons. Natural time exists beyond clock time, which frequently blocks impulses from essence that aid in fulfillment.

passion – what gets you excited in a spiritual sense; how essence works through your intuition to realize your desires.

Personal God – see *essence*.

policing in love – to provide fearless and respectful actions towards another that help them realize more fulfilling options.

pray – to engage your best reasoning and intuition to meditate into the space of non-reasoning. Prayers done before sleep help you assimilate the day's events, calm your mind, and lull you into the dreamspace where you will obtain specific help from essence.

probabilities – the vast expanse of fields in which you exist, and in which your every choice has an effect on the outcome of every event in your life and in those around you. Every action has probabilities built in, and every situation can go in any direction at any time, no matter how improbable it may be.

---

[25] See the Rest in Rose practice on page 192.

probable selves – versions of you who simultaneously experience alternate probabilities and paths in a variety of time-space dimensions.

remembrance – the sense of essence or soul nature that many individuals have lost touch with, but realize when they live in their way of spirit.

respect – the need to attract fondness in a most basic way that promotes response-ability. When you respect someone, you become familiar with them in subtle and profound ways.

response-ability – the ability for individuals to enjoy the responses to and consequences of the actions they choose.

Rest in Rose – a meditative practice to help you sense the fealing tone with Rose so that you may more easily do so with your own essence.[26]

senxuality – a sense of combined sexuality and sensuality that provides a deep connection with spirit.

shadow self – a necessary aspect of self that brings focus to thoughts and actions that conflict with your desires so that you may address them. Both *shadow inflation* and *shadow deflation* invalidate your own power and perpetuate suffering.

Shadow inflation happens when you think that you can't get what you want and project onto others who seem to have the power to do so. *Shadow deflation* happens when you project your dislike of your own perceived flaws onto another.

---

[26] See the Rest in Rose practice on page 192.

shift in consciousness – the global mass event in which individuals experience remembrance of essence. The frameworks for understanding and assisting individuals through this transition are being provided by Rose and other energy personality essences.

sonter – to breathe in your essence self in order to find your best, most authentic self in every moment.[27]

soul – see *essence*.

wants – what your ego thinks will bring you happiness, which may or may not be a true desire.

way of spirit – the most fulfilling course for your life, guided by your intent.

works – creative expressions guided by your intent.

Youniverse – the combination of your ego, essence, and All That Is, which is here to remind you that you never have to feal alone.

---

[27] See the Sonter (Breathe in Essence) practice on page 191.

Index

About the Author

Joanne Helfrich is an author, speaker, and guide who channels the essence of Rose.

She has authored essays, educational programs, and lectured nationally on personal and cultural transformation. She advocates channelling as an innate human intelligence, and has studied and promoted channelled information, including the Seth Material, Elias Forum, and Kris Chronicles. Her teachers include Dr. Don Beck (**spiraldynamics.net**), Ken Wilber (**integrallife.com**), and Matthew Fox (**matthewfox.org**).

In 2007, Joanne began her energy exchange with the essence of Rose (**thewayofspirit.com**). Along with partners Paul M. Helfrich and C.W.E. Johnson, she serves the growing international community that explores the practical applications of *conscious creation*—the many ways we create body, mind, and spirit within self, culture, and nature. For more information, visit **newworldview.com**.

Joanne lives in Topanga, California, with Paul and their cats, Rumi and Maya.

www.ingramcontent.com/pod-product-compliance
Lightning Source LLC
Chambersburg PA
CBHW060027100426
42740CB00010B/1630